YOUR STRENGTHS BLUEPRINT:

How to be Engaged, Energized, and Happy at Work

Michelle McQuaid & Erin Lawn

Author's Note: The names and identifying details of some of the people portrayed in this book have been changed.

Your Strengths Blueprint: How to be Engaged, Energized, and Happy at Work

Authors: Michelle McQuaid and Erin Lawn

Version 2.0

PO Box 230 Albert Park, VIC, 3206 Australia

ABN: 88094250503

www.michellemcquaid.com

Email: chelle@michellemcquaid.com

Design: That's Creative!

Typesetting: That's Creative!

Editing: First Editing

ISBN: 978-0-9872714-1-9

For Patrick, Charlie, and Jamie who are always willing to look for the true, the good, and the possible in me. And for Martin Seligman, Chris Peterson, Neal and Donna Mayerson, and each of the relentless researchers featured in this book whose commitment to discovering how we bring out the best in people opens up new possibilities in the ways we work and live.

Michelle

For my mum and dad, who have inspired me to dream, and filled me with the courage to believe in my strengths. And for Natalie Brain, Lea Waters, and Gavin Slemp, whose passion, kindness, and mentorship has sparked and nurtured my love for the study of human flourishing.

Erin

Contents

Foreword

The Adventure of the Positive-Strengths Revolution

By David L. Cooperrider

Life is either a daring adventure or nothing.

Helen Keller

***

I love the word adventure. It invites two seemingly opposite experiences: sensational excitement and disorienting risk. The excitement is obviously easy to embrace and understand, for we thrill to the adventurous moment including the novelty of unexplored pathways, expansive vistas, and sense of the possible. Explorers love adventure. However there is also the other side of authentic adventure. It can lead to the shock of new awareness. And even when the shock is positive, it can challenge deeply rooted assumptions of the status quo. Positive dislodgement of certainty can alter our lives, sometimes forever, and also in just an instant. An adventure always involves risk.

The same is true of big ideas—especially those that can enter our lives with no going back—and that is what this precious volume is all about. What this book by Michelle McQuaid and Erin Lawn does, perhaps better than any other I've seen, is to bring three revolutions into one unified, applied focus. Marcus Buckingham was perhaps the first to notice that someday these three could come together seamlessly, to provide all of us with a coherent set of mindsets and tools that can span the domains of family life, business and management, and individual psychology.[i] And what precisely did he notice? In his tracing of it there were three core contributions or resonant threads: (1) "The strengths revolution in management" articulated early on in Peter Drucker's 1966 management theory on *The Effective Executive*;[ii] (2) next, there was the call and vision in the field of organization development for an Appreciative Inquiry into Organizational Life (Cooperrider and Srivastva, 1987);[iii] and then (3) there was the comprehensive invitation to the field of psychology for a radical reversal; instead of a science pre-occupied by what's wrong with the human being, there would be a vast re-focusing into studies of the good life, the meaningful life, and the flourishing life, that is, the christening of the field of positive psychology (Seligman and Csikszentmihalyi, 2000.)[iv] What was emerging, argued Buckingham, was a richer and more complex web of mutually reinforcing ideas and solutions than anyone could have ever imagined.

When you fuse the word "positive" from the field of positive psychology, with word "strengths" from the emergence of strengths-based management, it may be no exaggeration to say that the premises, tools, and the across-the-board opportunities of what we might call the positive-strengths revolution might well be, as Harvard's Howard Gardner declared it, "the most far reaching development in the human sciences of the past half century." Only time will tell of course, yet one can see something of a re-birth, of whole disciplines breaking out anew. Alfred North Whitehead, the bold philosopher of his day, spoke in unforgettable terms about what he called *The Adventure of Ideas*, thrilling times when new fields are born, eras defined, and profound shifts in foundational beliefs are unleashed, all through the power of ideas.

In my view, the positive-strengths revolution is one of those adventures. And remember what I said at the outset? Explorations have a way of entering our lives with no going back. So are you wondering what this tiny little book can do for you? Yes, it will draw you in. And because you will love it and it will send you forward on a powerful yet simple pathway to your best life, you will never turn back.

The signature of this wonderful volume by McQuaid and Lawn is how it draws you in so easily into the science of human strengths and the discovery and deployment of your own life-giving strengths, including the well-rooted dreams they inspire. Research findings, instead of being dry and inert, are presented throughout with delicate precision and joyful clarity—and *just enough* for those who want the actual business case, the theories and data on human flourishing, the leadership case, and the case for positive change. But the parts of this book that I found most magnetic and alluring were in the spheres of everyday application. The personal storytelling of Michelle McQuaid, for example, brings everything into special focus because the storytelling is honest, heartfelt, and real. You cannot help but reflect on your own life as the authors narrate their own transformations and journeys. Moreover, the *playsheets* are powerful because they are explicitly designed and embedded in hope theory itself: the exercises cultivate willpower and waypower, and both are essential, in perfect combination.

So can you articulate your unique strengths—those patterns of thinking, feeling, or behaving that, when exercised, will excite, energize, and engage you? Do you know how to play to those strengths every single day, no matter what your job, and how building them will send waves of energy and excellence into your career, elevate your health, and create more hope, inspiration, and joy? Do you know how a strengths-designed life correlates with full spectrum flourishing and flow, positive relationships, and more peak experiences in arenas you value most? As McQuaid and Lawn so lucidly sum up: "Your strengths are your multiplier. Your strengths magnify you…they represent *you* at your best."

Right now this book is your doorway. Step into the experience. Treasure your curiosity. Be courageous. It's time to enter the adventure of the positive-strengths way of life, *and then see what happens*!

David L. Cooperrider
Weatherhead School of Management
Case Western Reserve University &
The David L. Cooperrider Center for Appreciative Inquiry
Champlain College, Burlington Vermont

Introduction

By Michelle McQuaid

Have you ever been asked to do something at work that you didn't really want to do? Have you ever found yourself coming up with all sorts of reasons to delay or put off a dreaded task? Perhaps it's something you haven't done before, and you're really not sure you can pull it off. Or maybe you just aren't that excited about spending time completing that particular activity. Or, in your mind, your boss may have gone completely mad!

A few years ago, I found myself in this exact situation.

My boss had asked me to take on what most people in our organization considered an impossible task—to reposition our brand. It was a job I didn't want to do for a whole lot of good reasons.

While most of my career had been in branding roles, I'd spent the last year completing my masters in applied positive psychology with the field's founder, Professor Martin Seligman. Positive psychology, or the scientific study of human flourishing, explores evidence-based approaches to help people feel happier, to be more engaged, to have better relationships, to find more meaning, and accomplish the things that matter to them most. You see, after more than a decade in senior leadership roles around the world, it had become increasingly clear to me that traditional approaches to managing people like command-and-control, and even empower-and-track, were failing to deliver the desired business results. Fascinated by how to consistently bring out the best in people within organizations, I was ready to apply all I'd learnt in my studies by moving into the area of human resources. This is why the idea of spending another year in a marketing role—where I felt like I'd already achieved all I ever wanted—held no appeal at all.

In addition, the organization had already tried to change its brand a number of times—with each failure more disheartening than the last. It wasn't that talented people hadn't made valiant efforts. Honestly, what we did as an organization was a little boring, and the organization generally lacked the appetite to make what we did more interesting or exciting.

To top it all off, the repositioning attempt I was being asked to lead had a small team, a tiny budget, and a tight deadline. Of course! Not exactly a recipe for success.

Unfortunately, in order to take the next step in my career and land the human resource job of my dreams, not only did I need to deliver this project, I also had to exceed everyone's expectations. How was I going to pull it off?

Luckily, through my studies in applied positive psychology, I had all the latest scientific theories about how to flourish—even in challenging situations— at my fingertips. This was my opportunity to see if the theories—such as positive emotions, strengths-based leadership, gratitude, growth mindsets, and hope—could be applied in the real world by drawing on every tested tool I'd uncovered. The results of what unfolded, and the growing body of research upon which positive psychology is founded, is a tale every employee and workplace should consider when it comes to improving individual, team, and organizational performance.

In just nine short months, not only was my team able to deliver what was required on time and on budget, but we exceeded every independent measure of success that had been set for employee engagement, customer satisfaction, and brand differentiation. There was nothing expensive or difficult in our approach; we simply learned to value and work to our *strengths*—those things we were good at and enjoyed doing in our work. For example, we channeled our strength of *curiosity* to find more effective ways to communicate; we unleashed our strength of *creativity* to better connect with people's hopes; we focused on our strength of *gratitude* to attract more resources and supporters; and we leveraged our strength of *hope* to excite people about what was possible. Leaders within the organization still cite this project as one of the most successful transformational changes ever implemented.

As a result, I scored my promotion, a whopping big pay raise, and the chance to craft the human resources job of my dreams. But what took me most by surprise was how much I enjoyed working on this project which I had initially dreaded, and how easy the seemingly 'impossible' became when I finally invested in my own and others' strengths.

Best of all, each of my team members still describe this project as one of the highlights of their careers. At first, they worried that the idea of focusing on their strengths rather than their weaknesses was some kind of new management trap, but their concerns quickly faded when they realized they were able to achieve better results by doing more of what they did best. They continue to use this approach to this day and teach others to do the same.

You might be wondering how a small and simple change can truly work. Well the good news is, the outcomes we achieved are not unique. As you'll see throughout this book, a growing body of research suggests that when we work from our strengths, it makes our goals easier to achieve, it lowers our levels of stress, and it improves our wellbeing. People who have the opportunity to do what they do best each day at work—even for just part of the day—are up to six times more engaged in their jobs. In teams where most people get to use their strengths regularly, staff turnover has been found to be lower, productivity to be higher, and customers to be more satisfied.

Does this sound like something you, your team, or your organization might need? Are you ready to make your work just a little bit easier and a lot more enjoyable? Would you like to be able to unleash the potential of the people in your team? Do you want to make your effort to achieve your business goals of employee engagement, customer satisfaction, and profitability more effective? Then this book is your blueprint to discovering, developing, and delivering on your strengths at work.

If you're new to the idea of using your strengths at work, then Part A of this book, "Knowing the What and Why of Strengths," will give you everything you need to understand why more and more organizations are turning to strength-development approaches for their employees. You'll understand exactly what is meant by terms like *strengths, character strengths*, and *talents*. And, by helping you understand how your brain works when you're at your best, you'll have the foundational knowledge that's required to confidently develop your strengths in your role, or within your organization, to achieve the results you most desire at work.

If you've already completed a strengths survey such as *StrengthsFinder*, the *Values in Action (VIA) Survey* or *Realise2*, but aren't sure what to do next, then Part B of this book, "Creating Your Strengths-Development Plan," gives you a practical and playful step-by-step guide to help you feel engaged, energized, and happy at work no matter what your job description says. Based on my years of experience drawing on tested positive psychology practices and applying these ideas in real organizations, you'll discover how you're already using your strengths. You'll also have a clear vision of what success looks like, learn how to map a busy-proof pathway to get you there, and find ways to take the first steps toward using your strengths more each day at work.

If you have been playing to your strengths for a while, then Part C of this book, "Building on Your Strengths," offers ideas for using your strengths to shape your career, improve your relationships, and bring out the best in your teams. Based on the approaches I've used for more than 6,500 employees to embed strengths into organizational relationships, processes, and systems, you'll find all the examples and templates you need to make strength-development approaches a way of life for your team.

To help you navigate through Parts A to C, you'll find several *play sheets* along the way which have been designed as small, practical-to-implement changes that can make a real difference in your life if you do the work. You'll also find that in the *case in point* sections, I share my own personal experiences to help you see what the various theories and strategies actually look like when they're applied in the real-world of work. Finally, the Appendix at the back of the book provides you with a profile of each of the twenty-four character strengths, so that you can better understand your VIA Survey results and uncover simple suggestions for developing these particular strengths at work.

You can read this book from cover to cover, but feel free to dive into the section that best meets your needs. Wherever you start, don't read this book as a theoretical exercise, as that would be a waste of your strengths. Rather, use the play sheets to *take action* after reading each chapter so you can apply these ideas and really test out the science. .

Ready to start?

PART A

Knowing the What & Why of Strengths

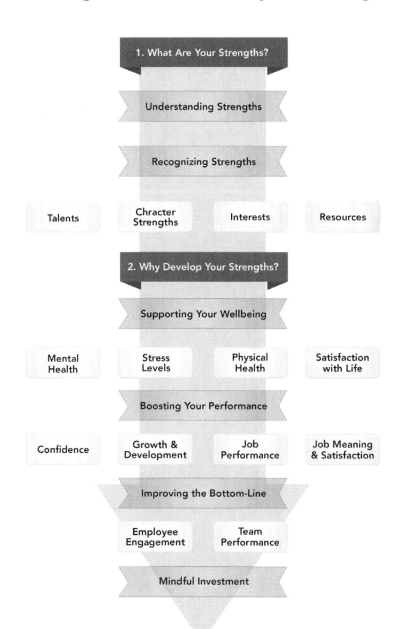

1. What Are Your Strengths?

Understanding Strengths

Recognizing Strengths

| Talents | Chracter Strengths | Interests | Resources |

2. Why Develop Your Strengths?

Supporting Your Wellbeing

| Mental Health | Stress Levels | Physical Health | Satisfaction with Life |

Boosting Your Performance

| Confidence | Growth & Development | Job Performance | Job Meaning & Satisfaction |

Improving the Bottom-Line

| Employee Engagement | Team Performance |

Mindful Investment

CHAPTER 1

What Are Your Strengths?

C an you name your top five strengths? You know, those things you're good at and actually enjoy? If you're struggling to come up with five strengths, don't despair. As it turns out, most of us have no idea what our strengths actually are, never mind how to use them in our jobs![1]

The first step in your strength-development blueprint is to understand what comprises a strength and how its different elements work. For example, do you want to focus on *what* you're doing in your job, or *how* you're doing your job? Feeling confident about the different elements that comprise your strengths gives you the power to focus on the tools and activities that will deliver the best results for the situation you're in at work, and enable you to achieve the outcomes you want.

In this chapter, we'll give you all the background you need to understand exactly what a strength is and the different kinds of strengths you can draw on to make your work more engaging, enjoyable, and energizing. This way, you'll have a clear understanding of what your strengths are, which will make it easier to find ways to develop them in Part B.

Understanding Strengths

In its simplest form, a strength is *something you are good at and enjoy doing*. Yes, it's that basic, and it's all you need to remember when it comes to strength-development approaches at work.

If you're more scientifically minded, you'll be comforted to know that this definition is grounded in a growing body of research from leading academics such as the late Professor Chris Peterson, Dr. Robert Biswas-Diener, Dr.

Alex Linley, and many others. Based on their work to date, a more scientific definition of a strength goes something like this:

> *Strengths are patterns of thinking, feeling, or behaving that, when exercised, will excite, engage, and energize you, and allow you to perform at your optimum level.*[2]

What does this mean exactly? Let's consider each part in more detail:

1. **Strengths refer to your particular *patterns of thoughts, feelings, and actions.***

   Without going into the intricate nuances of neuroscience, your every thought, feeling, and action occur because you have billions of cells in your brain called "neurons" which light up and send messages to each other. Over time as you repeat particular thoughts, feelings, and behaviors, these cells become interconnected in every which way to form a complex set of neural pathways, making it easier and faster for the messages to travel through your brain. You might have heard the phrase, "Neurons that fire together, wire together," and this is literally what's happening inside your head. Using your strengths seems second nature or automatic because of the way our brains work.[3]

   You can put this process to the test right now.

   Grab a pen and write your first and last name with your dominant hand. If you're right-handed, you'll use your right hand, and if you're left-handed, you'll use your left hand.

   When you have finished this, swap the pen into your non-dominant hand—the hand you don't usually write with—and write your first and last name once more.

   Notice any differences?

   Provided you're not ambidextrous, chances are you found writing your name with your dominant hand fairly easy. It didn't require too much attention or effort, and you were probably reasonably happy with the result. In other words, it's a neurological strength for you. This is because you've practiced writing your name again and again and again with that hand over the years. As a result, you've built up a neural pathway in your brain that supports the efficient and effective execution of this behavior.

However, writing your name with your non-dominant hand was probably a bit harder, took more effort, and you might not have been as happy with the result. This is because you haven't repeated this pattern of action frequently enough to build a strong neural pathway to make this behavior easy. Consequently, this is more of a weakness than a strength.

As you've probably already discovered, just because you can do something easily—like write with your dominant hand—it doesn't necessarily mean you want to spend more time doing it at work. This brings us to the second part of our strengths definition.

2. **The opportunity to exercise your strengths will be** *exciting, engaging, and energizing* **to you.**

Using your strengths should also feel good. Strengths aren't just things you can do well; they're also things you look forward to doing. You feel energized and absorbed while doing them. And, afterwards, you're left feeling invigorated and fulfilled. For example, Michelle's strength of curiosity means she loves immersing herself in a new book or article where she can discover new approaches for bringing out the best in other people. And, Erin's strength of *perseverance* means she feels truly satisfied when she can follow a task through all the way to completion.

Your strengths are a reflection of your interests and passions, and they provide an opportunity for you to express yourself and what's important to you in an authentic and balanced way. That's why when you use your strengths, you feel like the "real me" is coming through.[4]

Dr. Robert Biswas-Diener, renowned in positive psychology for his research on strengths with Massai warriors in Africa, explains that a person might be good at organizing themselves, being persuasive, or comforting others—but if it's not something that gives them an emotional boost or a little burst of energy, then it is probably not a strength.[5]

3. **Exercising your strengths allows you to *perform at your peak.***

Our understanding of the application of strengths has also been greatly aided by Marcus Buckingham, a researcher, best-selling author, and business consultant, who found that despite sixty-one percent of people believing we grow the most in our areas of weakness, we actually experience our greatest learnings and successes when we use our strengths.[6]

Why? Well, here our definition of strengths comes full circle. First, it takes your brain far less effort to build on the neural pathways you already have than to create new ones. Secondly, when you're engaged, energized, and enjoying what you're doing, you're more optimistic, courageous, and resilient in the face of obstacles and setbacks. Your strengths are your multiplier. Your strengths magnify you. In other words, your strengths are named as such because they represent *you at your best.*

If the above three definitional components seem like a lot to remember, just go back to where we started: Your strengths are things you're good at and enjoy doing. They're how your brain is wired to perform at its best.

Recognizing Strengths

Now that you understand what a strength is, let's broaden our definition to distinguish between the different types of strengths you may find yourself using. Dr. Ryan Niemiec, a psychologist and one of the world's leading strength teachers, explains that your strengths may include your talents, your character strengths, your interests, and/or your resources.[7]

Talents

The father of strengths-based psychology, Dr. Donald Clifton, spent more than forty years showing up at work each morning to study "what's right with people." Based at the University of Nebraska, his research started in the 1950s, and after interviewing more than ten million people, he defined strengths as, "The consistent near perfect performance in an activity that led to high levels of achievement."[8]

Clifton's research led him to argue that there are three principles for living a strong life.

1. For an activity to be a strength, you must be able to do it consistently. This means you can demonstrate it time and time again, implying that you can do it repeatedly, happily, and successfully.

2. You don't have to have a strength for every aspect of your role to excel. Rather than being well rounded or dealt the perfect hand, you can make the best of what you have and be sharp in the use of your strengths.

3. You will excel only by maximizing your strengths, never by fixing your weaknesses. This doesn't mean you ignore your weaknesses; rather, you manage around your weaknesses by capitalizing on your strengths.[9]

Clifton believed that when the goal was to produce a consistent, near-perfect performance, practice didn't necessarily make perfect. Instead, he argued that developing a strength requires natural *talents* that cannot be cultivated after a certain age.[10] This is a central and distinctive component of Clifton's conceptualization of strengths.

Clifton concluded that the key to building a genuine strength is to identify your dominant talents. Your talents refer to the natural way you think, feel, and behave, which can be applied in a productive way. For example, people with the talent of *Analytical* like to search for reasons and causes; people with the talent of *Communications* easily put their thoughts into words; and people with the talent of *Relator* enjoy close relationships with others. Once you've discovered these talents, the next step is to amplify them, through your investment in acquiring more factual knowledge, real-life experience, and building your skills.[11]

Finally, it's important to note that talents are non-moral. They are valued for the tangible experiences they create. This means that when you use your talents, you're *extrinsically* motivated by the prospective recognition and rewards that will come from their application. Talents also generally relate more to "what" you like to do, and are a reflection of your abilities.[12]

Character Strengths

Professor Martin Seligman, one of the founders of positive psychology, proposes that a fulfilling life requires more than just mere achievement. After many healthy discussions with Clifton about what comprises a strength, Seligman and his dear friend and colleague the late Professor Chris Peterson, decided to focus their research on "character" rather than "talent."

Seligman and Peterson decided to regard good character as a family of positive dispositions, like *perspective, teamwork, kindness,* and *humor.* As a result, they defined *character strengths* as the psychological ingredients— processes or mechanisms—that define morally valued virtues.[13]

To say that a character strength is morally valued is an important qualification. Unlike a talent, character strengths are valued in their own right and not for the tangible outcomes that they produce. Consequently, character strengths are *intrinsically* motivating; you'll use them regardless of whether anyone recognizes or pays you for them.[14]

While your character strengths are trait-like in that you can see the individual differences between people, they're also shaped by your settings and are thus capable of change. For example, character strengths like *bravery, fairness,* and *kindness* can be built on frail foundations, but with enough practice, persistence, good teaching, and dedication, they can strengthen and flourish. Michelle—as an introvert who's more comfortable spending time thinking of ideas inside her own head rather than connecting with other people—has significantly improved her relationships with others over time by exploring, testing, and ritualizing acts of kindness. Building character strengths and using them in daily life is not about learning, training, or conditioning; it's about discovery, creation, and ownership.[15] Perhaps this is why character strengths are generally more about "how" we like to do things and are a reflection of the values we hold.[16]

You'll note that in the Appendix at the back of this book, we've provided you with a profile of each of the twenty-four character strengths that researchers have identified. In Chapter 3 of this book, you'll learn more about how these character strengths were uncovered, and how they are measured.

Interests

Our natural and innate urges take the form of the interest in certain topics and activities that we're passionate about and driven to pursue. These *interests* are what we enjoy doing and ultimately determine where our attention goes. As a result, recent research suggests that, when it comes to cultivating our strengths, our interests are an important moderator in what we're willing to practice and the success we're able to achieve.[17]

Dr. Alex Linley, one of the world's leading researchers on developing strengths, suggests that two of the best ways to spot your interests are to:

- Notice what you naturally pay attention to, as you're more likely to focus on things that are playing to your strengths.

- Tune in to what motivates you, and the activities that you do simply for the love of doing them, as they are likely to be working from your strengths.[18]

Of course, your interests will change over time, so it's important to keep tuning in to the answers to these questions and noticing what's claiming your attention. For example, at the start of Michelle's career, she was passionately interested in how to communicate well with others—leading her to branding and marketing roles. Later, she became interested in how to bring out the best in people within workplaces—leading her to human resources roles.

Resources

In order to truly develop the neural pathways that represent your strengths—be it your talents or your character strengths—you need to nourish them with the right external resources. *Factual knowledge, experiential knowledge,* and *networks* are three of the most important resources that researchers have discovered to date.[19]

- **Factual knowledge:** This refers to the information that you need in order to perform any task well. Think of factual knowledge resources as any of the formal or informal learning bases from which you can extract useful information.[20] Examples of this may include undertaking a course or a degree, attending a conference, watching a documentary, or even reading widely. The information contained in this book is another good example of a knowledge resource, as you'll be able to use the concepts you learn in order to fine-tune the application of your strengths.

- **Experiential knowledge:** This is the information you gain through engaging in action. Experiential knowledge allows you to put your strengths into practice and obtain feedback. This helps you to discover where you're using your strengths well, and where you have room to improve; thus allowing you to fine-tune your application.[21] Examples of this might include the opportunity to work in a team, speak in front of an audience, or work within a tight deadline. Each experience provides you with the chance to learn in a way that you can't do by just picking up a book.

- **Networks:** Your social networks are the group(s) of people around you who provide support, encouragement, and an appreciation of your strengths. This might include teams within your organization, members of your family, strength coaches and academics, or anyone else you know who is undertaking a similar journey to you. Your networks are valuable because they offer a friendly stage upon which to play with your strengths and build your confidence. Furthermore, exposure to these networks often provides further opportunities to access knowledge and experiences you couldn't access alone.

Like most science that explores human behavior, discovering exactly what comprises a strength is a little bit messy and there is still plenty we're learning. Remember, at the most basic level, all you really need to know is that a strength is something you're good at and enjoy doing. To find out why this matters when it comes to ways you can improve your work, please refer to Chapter 2.

Case In Point

By Michelle McQuaid

I thrive on taking an average idea and making it excellent. Even as a child, I was constantly inventing new and better ways to improve the games we played and to deliver on school assignments. These early examples of my talent to *"maximize"*—to transform something strong into something superb—eventually steered me toward business roles focused on creating and driving change in large organizations.

You see, I'm at my best when I'm figuring out how to maximize the way something works. For example, as the global brand director for one firm, I relished the opportunity to pilot ideas in one country, and then build upon this model to roll the tested campaign out around the world. Once it became "business-as-usual," I was no longer engaged and energized by the work, and I realized that it was time to seek the next challenge to keep improving on my achievements. "Maximizing" is what I love to do at work.

Of course, not every job I've taken has given me an outlet for this talent. When I left my global brand role, I became the Australian brand director for the same firm. I'd moved home for family reasons, so I needed a job and was grateful to be given one. But as I mentioned in the introduction of this book, I wasn't very excited about this role, as there was little business appetite for my talent of "maximizing". Limited by what I could do in my job each day, I instead focused my energy on *how* I went about it.

I've discovered that my most fulfilling days in life are when I learn something new about how to bring out the best in myself and others, and have the chance to share what I've discovered. This is my character strength of *"curiosity"* in action, and it means I truly enjoy exploring new ideas and approaches. It's a strength I'll use whether or not anybody pays me or recognizes me for it, because it makes life enjoyable for me.

Faced with a role I dreaded, my character strength of curiosity became my lifeline. When I first arrived at work each morning, I'd spend at least ten minutes indulging my curiosity strength by learning something new—like how having fun at work impacts productivity—to help me better manage my team and the project we were delivering. Then, each Friday I'd send my boss an email with 'the three things I learnt this week', as well as the thoughts it had prompted for how we could apply these improvements in our team. It wasn't part of my job description, but this one opportunity to play to my strengths ensured I remained engaged, energized, and enjoying a role where my talents weren't fully occupied. "Curiosity" is how I love to work.

Finally, the resources I can use to nurture both my talents and my character strengths have been instrumental in my growth. I've used the formal knowledge gained from my masters in applied positive psychology to bolster my talent for maximizing strengths, and to direct my curiosity to material that enables me to learn more about human flourishing. And while formal learning opportunities are great, there's nothing like the experiential knowledge that comes from leading a team to discover how, and if, theoretical ideas on wellbeing work for people who are knee-deep in organizational challenges. But what continues to accelerate my strengths-development more than any other mechanism is the network—or tribe—of people who nourish my interests, encourage my applications, and give me honest feedback so I can continue improving.

These are some of my talents, character strengths, and resources. While each can stand-alone, I've found my work and life is far more fulfilling when I find the places that these three types of strengths overlap and enhance each other.

CHAPTER 2

Why Develop Your Strengths?

Now that you understand what a strength comprises, it's time to turn your attention to the next question: Why should you care about developing your strengths at work? After all, using your strengths sounds like a nice idea, but is there any real benefit to you, your team, or your organization?

Researchers have been investigating the benefits of developing strengths for some time, and a growing body of evidence suggests that when you have the chance to do what you do best more frequently at work, and to develop your strengths, it improves your individual wellbeing, performance, and your organization's bottom line. There are also some occasions where it appears that using your strengths may not be in your best interest, and it's important you're aware of these situations before you embark on your strength-development journey.

You may wish to simply skim this chapter, reading the *Supporting Your Wellbeing, Boosting Your Performance, Improving The Bottom Line* and *Mindful Investment* overviews and the corresponding Business Case research summaries. Each of these sections will give you an overview of what researchers have found to date about the benefits of developing your strengths. If your primary interest is in how your strengths might help you— and perhaps your team—to be more engaged, energized and happy at work, then these summaries will likely answer all the questions you currently have, without overwhelming you with scientific detail.

For complete transparency however, we believe it is also important to offer you easy access to the research on which these conclusions are based. This is why below each summary, you'll find detailed accounts of each study. If you are comfortable with academic research, reviewing the studies in more detail will provide you with further insights into what is actually known about developing strengths—and what is still to be discovered. We particularly recommend that students and practitioners of positive psychology and strength-based approaches familiarize themselves with how this research is being conducted.

Let us acknowledge upfront that much is still being learned, and no one study presents the perfect insight or answer on how developing strengths can improve your work and your life. The mechanisms and outcomes of human behavior are not simple, clear-cut processes with absolute answers, as so much depends upon the group of people studied, the time period in which they're measured, and researchers' abilities to control or account for a host of external factors. As such, we urge you to view the outcomes reported in each study as suggestions and possibilities, based on the researchers' chosen methodology.

Supporting Your Wellbeing

Work-related stress is a growing problem around the world that affects not only the health and wellbeing of employees, but also the productivity of organizations. Long hours, heavy workloads, job insecurity, and conflicts with our bosses and colleagues cause many of us to feel anxious, overwhelmed, tired, and in some cases depressed and physically ill.

Of course, intermittent periods of stress or anxiety at work are not a bad thing. In the blink of an eye, stress triggers an amazing set of bodily responses. Our blood moves from our brains to our arms and legs to get us moving; our adrenal glands release surges of adrenaline and cortisol to fire up our energy levels; our interest in food and sex takes a backseat; endorphins are released to blunt any pain; and scores of neurotransmitters put our brains on high alert.[1] In fact, performance peaks under the heightened activation that comes with moderate levels of stress.[2]

The challenge comes when stress at work is no longer measured in intermittent moments, but in hours, days, and sometimes even in months or years. We simply weren't built to handle consistently large amounts of stress, and over prolonged periods, stress changes the way our brain and body operate. An overload of stress makes it difficult for us to think quickly and creatively, to learn new things, to practice self-control, and to connect well with others. When stress becomes chronic, it eventually shifts our brain chemistry toward anxiety or depression, and it affects our immune response and cardiovascular functioning, elevating the risk of colds, diseases, strokes, and heart attacks.[3]

Fortunately, stress is a *psychological* reaction that triggers physiological responses in your body, which means you have more control over your stress levels than you might think. It isn't your deadlines, your boss's expectations, or the person who drives you crazy at the office that's stressful. Indeed, there is actually no objective stress in the world—just a lot of stressful thoughts.[4]

The studies below suggest that developing your strengths can be an effective means of combating stress. When it comes to wellbeing and the ability to individually flourish at work, not only do people who use their strengths report lower levels of stress, they also report higher levels of happiness, lower levels of depression, better physical health, and higher levels of satisfaction with their lives. The more hours each day people use their strengths, the less likely they are to experience worry, stress, anger, sadness, or physical pain; and the more likely they are to have ample energy, feel well-rested, be happy, smile or laugh a lot, learn something interesting, and be treated with respect. It appears that developing your strengths is good for your mental and physical health, both of which make it easier to navigate the natural highs and lows we all experience at work.

The Business Case for Wellbeing

- **People who use their strengths more are happier.**

  Studies have found they report lower levels of depression, higher levels of vitality, and good mental health.

- **People who use their strengths more experience less stress.**

  Studies have found they report higher levels of positivity; and in particular the character strengths of *kindness, social intelligence, self-regulation,* and *perspective* appear to create a buffer against the negative effects of stress and trauma.

The Business Case for Wellbeing (cont.)

- **People who use their strengths more feel healthier and have more energy.**

  Studies have found that greater endorsement of character strengths is associated with a number of healthy behaviors including leading an active life, pursuing enjoyable activities, and eating well.

- **People who use their strengths more feel more satisfied with their lives.**

  Studies have found individuals who are satisfied with life are good problems-solvers, show better work performance, tend to be more resistant to stress and experience better physical health.

Mental Health

Martin Seligman and his colleagues found that one way to combat the kind of stress that lowers happiness and can lead to depression was by focusing your attention on what is within, rather than beyond, your control. More than 500 people volunteered to participate in the research through Seligman's website, www.authentichappiness.org. Participants were predominantly well-educated, Caucasian, "average" income earners, and were aged between thirty-five and fifty-four years. Before taking the intervention tests, participants were measured for their initial levels of depression and happiness. It was found that participants, on average, indicated that they were initially mildly depressed.

Participants were then randomly assigned to complete one of four exercises over a period of one week. Three of these were "happiness" exercises; designed to either build gratitude, increase awareness of what was most positive about themselves, or identify their character strengths. The fourth was a placebo-control exercise, where participants were asked to journal about early childhood memories. After one week of completing their given exercises, participants were later given follow-up tests for their depression and happiness levels at one week, one month, three month, and six month intervals.

Results showed that regardless of their assigned exercise, participants—even those in the placebo-control group—were on average happier and less depressed at immediate post-test. At the six-month evaluation however, only two exercises continued to increase happiness and decrease depressive symptoms. The first was the daily gratitude exercise, in which participants spent the week writing down three things every night that went well during that day. The second was the strengths-development exercise, where participants completed a character strengths survey online and received individual feedback about their top five "signature" strengths, and then used these strengths in a new and different way every day for one week. The researchers found that due to the "fun" nature of these two exercises, participants continued to spontaneously practice these gratitude and strengths-development activities beyond the study's one-week intervention period. This is what enabled these two groups of participants to continue improving their happiness and lowering their depression levels up to six months after the initial intervention.[5]

Fabian Gander of the University of Switzerland, and his colleagues, aimed to replicate this finding with a non-English-speaking sample of more than 1,500 adults with a mean age of 44.87 years. Most participants were women, and over half had a university-level education. Like Seligman's study, participants were instructed to use their signature character strengths in a new way each day for one week. Once more, an increase in participants' happiness levels and a decrease in their depressive symptoms was found up to six months later.[6]

Dr. Jo Mitchell of Monash University and her colleagues also investigated whether a person's wellbeing could be influenced by instructing them to both identify and use their strengths. The research sample included 160 Australian adults with a mean age of thirty-seven years. Most participants were women who had completed a university-level education. All participants completed baseline measures for the Personal-Wellbeing Index, Satisfaction with Life Scale, Positive and Negative Affect Schedule, Depression Anxiety Stress Scale, and Orientations to Happiness.

Each participant was randomly assigned to one of three groups. Over three sessions, participants in the strengths intervention group identified and prioritized their strengths using a list of the twenty-four character strengths. These participants selected three of their top ten strengths to develop further in daily life over one week, and were provided with examples and an online downloadable diary to record and share their progress. Also over three sessions, participants in the problem-solving intervention group were introduced to a cognitive-behavioral approach to problem solving, and were asked to practice applying this model to a real life problem. They were each provided with an online downloadable diary to help them record and share their progress. Finally, participants in the placebo control group were given an abbreviated version of the problem-solving intervention, where they were neither asked to apply the information to a real life problem nor to complete any sharing or monitoring. All participants then completed post-test measures—immediately after intervention as well as three months later—for the Personal-Wellbeing Index, Satisfaction with Life Scale, Positive and Negative Affect Schedule, Depression Anxiety Stress Scale, and Orientations to Happiness.

The results showed that only the participants in the strengths intervention group experienced a significant increase in subjective wellbeing, and that these changes continued in an upward trajectory for at least three months. It's worth noting, however, that these improvements were in the cognitive (i.e. the way participants *thought* about life domains such as their standard of living, accomplishments, relationships, etc.) but not affective (i.e. *feeling* strong, alert, inspired) components of subjective wellbeing.[7]

Dr. Alex Linley and his colleague also found that the knowledge and use of one's strengths are significantly associated with feelings of happiness, wellbeing, and vitality.[8] Other studies specific to character strengths suggest that the development of strengths is highly correlated with good mental health[9] and a unique predictor of subjective wellbeing.[10]

Stress Levels

Professor Alex Wood at the University of Stirling and his colleagues found that people who use their strengths more report lower levels of stress. More than two hundred people, with an approximately equal number of men and women, were recruited to the sample. All participants had completed school, were thirty-two years–old on average, and were from a local English community.

Firstly, to establish a baseline, participants were asked to complete a series of measures including how frequently they were using their strengths, and their perceived levels of stress, vitality, and self-esteem. Participants were then re-tested on each of these measures both three and six months later to examine whether any changes in wellbeing occurred.

Re-test results showed that people who had reported greater use of their strengths at the outset had developed greater wellbeing over time. Specifically, at both three and six-month follow-ups, greater strengths use was related to higher self-esteem, vitality, and positivity, as well as lower perceived stress.[11]

With regard to specific character strengths, a growing group of researchers have been exploring whether particular strengths are more effective than others when it comes to improving your wellbeing. Currently, these studies suggest that the strengths of *kindness, social intelligence, self-regulation,* and *perspective* buffer against the negative effects of stress and trauma, thus preventing or limiting problems in their wake.[12] Other research has found that for people struggling with psychological disorders like anxiety or depression, the strengths of *appreciation of beauty and excellence,* and *love of learning* can help restore their sense of life satisfaction. [13]

Physical Health

Dr. Rene Proyer from the University of Zurich and his colleagues set out to understand whether the use of someone's strengths not only impacted their mental wellbeing, but their physical wellbeing as well. Their sample comprised 440 adults aged eighteen to seventy-five years, with the majority being German-speaking Swiss women who had attended university.

Using established scales, participants were asked to evaluate their own health status. This was found to be substantially related to external criteria such as the number of physician visits, the frequency with which they engaged in health-related behaviors (i.e. pursuing sports, wearing a seat belt, complying with medical prescriptions, avoiding consumption of nicotine, eating healthily, and maintaining personal hygiene) and their physical fitness. They also completed the VIA Survey to assess their 24 character strengths.

Results suggested that greater endorsement of character strengths was associated with a number of health behaviors. These included feeling healthy, leading an active way of life, the pursuit of enjoyable activities, healthy eating, and physical fitness. While the character strength of *self-regulation* had the highest association overall, the strengths of *curiosity, appreciation of beauty and excellence, gratitude, hope,* and *humor* also displayed strong connections with health behaviors.[14]

Professor Chris Peterson from the University of Michigan, and his colleagues, also found that in the case of physical illness, the character strengths of *bravery, kindness,* and especially *humor* helped restore a sense of satisfaction with life in the wake of a health crisis. They suggested that these three character strengths appear to help the seriously ill to keep going on with the rest of their life despite having poor health. *Bravery* perhaps helps us stare our own mortality in the face. *Kindness* heightens a state of empathy and the need for meaning and purpose. And *humor* undermines our fear and aids in a sense of relief and coping.[15]

Satisfaction with Life

Professor Nansook Park, from the University of Michigan, and her colleagues set out to discover whether particular character strengths show a stronger link to life satisfaction than other character strengths. Park notes that:

"Life satisfaction reflects an individual's appraisal of their life as whole. High life satisfaction correlates with the absence of psychological and social problems such as depression and dysfunctional relationships. Furthermore, individuals who are satisfied with life are good problems-solvers, show better work performance, tend to be more resistant to stress and experience better physical health."

Three samples of adult volunteers were recruited over the Internet, totaling more than five thousand participants. On average, the sample comprised female U.S. citizens, aged thirty-five to forty years.

Firstly, participants discovered their character strengths using the VIA Survey (see Chapter 3 of this book). Following this, they completed the Satisfaction with Life Scale by responding to statements on a seven-point Likert scale, such as: "If I could live my life over, I would change almost nothing".

Of the twenty-four character strengths, *hope, zest, gratitude, curiosity,* and *love* were substantially related to life satisfaction, while *modesty* and various intellectual strengths like *creativity, judgment, love of learning,* and *appreciation of beauty and excellence* were only weakly associated with life satisfaction.[16]

Further studies have also found similar results to those obtained by Park and colleagues. In one study, which included a sample of more than one thousand women, it was found that the character strengths of *hope* and *spirituality* were the best predictors of future life satisfaction.[17] Another study, which sampled more than three hundred Swiss adults, also reported that the character strengths of *hope, zest, curiosity, gratitude,* and *love* play key roles in connection with life satisfaction.[18] And, in a further study of more than eight hundred Croatian adults, the character strengths of *curiosity* and *zest* were consistently associated with lives of pleasure, engagement, and meaning.[19]

Interested in exploring whether these specific character strengths can be developed to improve satisfaction with life, Rene Proyer and his colleagues at the University of Switzerland gathered 178 German adults for their sample.

Participants were divided into three groups. The first group attended weekly training sessions and were assigned strength-development exercises for the character strengths of curiosity, gratitude, hope, and zest (for this study, *love* was replaced with *humor*), as these strengths were substantially related to life satisfaction in the previous studies. The second group attended weekly training sessions and were assigned strength-development exercises for the character strengths of *creativity, love of learning, judgment, and appreciation of beauty and excellence* (for this study, *humility* was replaced with *kindness*), as these strengths were least related to life satisfaction in the previous studies. The third group was waitlisted to complete the exercises after the study was over, but completed the same pre and post-test questionnaires at the same time periods to provide a control group. All participants completed the VIA Survey and Satisfaction with Life Scale two to four weeks before the training sessions started, and again two to four weeks after all sessions were completed.

The results showed that developing the character strengths which previous studies had shown to be highly related with life satisfaction significantly enhanced the first group's satisfaction with life. However, the researchers also found that, while not as statistically significant, developing the character strengths that previous studies had shown to be least related to life satisfaction still led to higher subjective gains in life satisfaction for the participants in group two versus the control group. This led researchers to conclude that developing any of the character strengths seems to be beneficial for people.[20]

In 2008, the Gallup Research Organization and Healthways (a global wellbeing company) merged decades of clinical, health leadership, and behavioral economics research to track and understand the key factors that drive wellbeing. Gallup conducted five hundred telephone interviews a day with Americans who were estimated to represent ninety-five percent of US households.

In the phone calls, researchers gathered the participants' perceptions of their wellbeing with respect to life evaluation, emotional health, physical health, healthy behavior, work environment, and basic access. One of the items measured for 'work environment' was the participant's ability to use their strengths.

Based on this data, Gallup reported that using one's strengths at work leads to improved health and wellness outcomes. The more hours each day that Americans were able to use their strengths to do what they do best, the less likely they were to experience worry, stress, anger, sadness, or physical pain, and the more likely they were to have ample energy, feel well-rested, be happy, smile or laugh regularly, learn something interesting, and be treated with respect.[21]

In fact, Gallup's global data also showed that people who had the opportunity to use their strengths at work were up to six times as likely to be engaged in their jobs and more than three times as likely to experience an excellent quality of life.[22] As a result, these people could enjoy a full forty-hour workweek, while those who did not have the opportunity to use their strengths were likely to get burned out after just twenty hours of work per week.[23]

Boosting Your Performance

When Freud was asked what a normal person should be able to do well, he replied, "Love and work." In 1959, Harvard psychologist Robert White's research found overwhelming evidence that people have a basic drive to make things happen. Babies take joy not just from looking at their toys, but flailing their arms to activate ringing bells, spinning wheels, and vibrating animals. Older children play make-believe games as they build cubby houses and embark on adventures to boost performance. And you can see a lack of drive in the weariness that often occurs when people stop working—be it from retirement, job loss, or no longer having a financial need to work. As humans, we have a basic psychological need for industry and mastering skills. White called this the "effectance motive" and believed that our drive to develop competence, through interacting with and controlling our environments, was a constant presence in our lives. This is why we so often get more pleasure from making progress toward our goals than we do from achieving them. As Shakespeare observed, "Joy's soul lies in the doing." [24]

The studies in this section suggest that developing your strengths can be an effective means of improving your individual performance at work. When it comes to unleashing your potential, knowing and using your strengths has been found to positively impact your self-belief, self-esteem, and confidence. Perhaps this is because building on your strengths—rather than focusing on your weaknesses—appears to provide a more effective pathway to growth and development, whilst being positively associated with key measures of job performance and your ability to find meaning in your work.

The Business Case for Performance

- **People who use their strengths more are more confident.**

  Studies have found that both strengths knowledge and strengths-use are significantly associated with self-efficacy, self-esteem, self-acceptance, and self-confidence.

- **People who use their strengths more experience faster growth and development.**

  Studies have found that positive self-monitoring and strengths building are particularly suited to circumstances when you're learning something new, something difficult, or something perceived as difficult.

- **People who use their strengths more are more creative and agile at work.**

  Studies have found that the feelings of authenticity, vitality and concentration created by developing strengths help people to better adapt to change, engage in more creative and proactive behaviors, pay more attention to detail, and work harder.

- **People who use their strengths more feel more satisfied and experience more meaning in their work.**

  Studies have found that people who use four or more of their top character strengths at work are more likely to experience job satisfaction, pleasure, engagement, and meaning in their work.

Confidence

In order to turn our thoughts into action and to build mastery, we need confidence. Mastery at work requires process and progress. It means inevitably encountering hurdles—sometimes overcoming them and sometimes failing, but always being willing to make the effort to learn and improve. Mastery cultivates an appetite for challenges, and when we master one thing, it gives us the confidence to try something else. It's about having resilience and not giving up.[25]

Reena Govindji and her colleagues at the Center for Applied Positive Psychology have explored how knowing and using your strengths impacts self-efficacy—the belief in your ability to succeed at something, and a common scientific conception of confidence. They gathered 214 college students with a mean age of 22.78 years. Sixty percent were women, enrolled in courses including psychology, science, humanities, law, and government and politics.

The participants completed a range of surveys including the General Self-efficacy Scale (a five-point Likert Scale that includes statements like, "In general, I think I can obtain outcomes that are important to me"), the Strengths Knowledge Scale (which assesses one's awareness and recognition of their strengths, simply defined as, "the things you are able to do well or best"), and the Strengths Use Scale (which assesses how much people use their strengths in a variety of settings, using a seven-point Likert scale for statements like, "My work gives me lots of opportunities to use my strengths").

Their results found that both strengths knowledge and strengths-use were significantly associated with self-efficacy.[26]

Gurpal Minhas, also from the Center for Applied Positive Psychology, has explored the relationship between the use of strengths and people's levels of self-esteem—the belief that we have value—which is another concept that overlaps with confidence. The sample comprised university administrators, who were predominantly women aged 36 years.

In the small study, which was conducted over a four-week period, participants were allocated at random to either develop a strength which they recognized and used readily (a realized strength), or a strength that was dormant (an unrealized strength). Both pre and post-test measures were taken of participants' levels of work engagement, psychological wellbeing, satisfaction with life and self-esteem.

The results found that self-esteem was significantly higher after developing either the realized or the unrealized strength. Not only did self-esteem increase, but engagement, satisfaction with life, and psychological wellbeing—specifically, environmental mastery and self-acceptance—were also improved.[27]

A final relevant finding comes from Gallup, who conducted follow-up surveys on almost five hundred readers of *Now, Discover Your Strengths* seventy-five days after these readers had completed the StrengthsFinder Survey. It was found that sixty percent of these participants agreed that they had improved their productivity by focusing on their strengths, and sixty-three percent agreed that their self-confidence had improved as a result of being educated about their strengths.[28]

Growth and Development

Professor Daniel Kirschenbaum of the University of Wisconsin-Madison and his colleagues set up an interesting experiment to illustrate the impact of building strengths in comparison to fixing weaknesses. The participants of this study were 133 women who bowled in a weekly league competition.

Participants were divided into the following groups. Those in the positive self-monitoring group were first given instruction on the seven key components of effective bowling (through a twenty to thirty-minute standardized team lesson from a professional bowler), and were then told to focus on all the things they effectively executed (their *strengths*) when they filled out their performance evaluation sheets at the end of each game. Participants in the negative self-monitoring group were also given this team lesson on how to bowl effectively, but were then told to focus on all the errors they made (*weaknesses*) when they filled out their evaluation sheets at the end of each game. Those in the instruction only group similarly received the lesson on how to bowl effectively, but were not encouraged to monitor their performance after each game. And finally, members of the control group were neither given any instruction nor any encouragement to monitor their performance. Across these four groups, participants were further divided into low-skill and high-skill bowlers. The expectation was that building upon one's strengths for the game would be helpful for low-skill bowlers, and that fixing one's weaknesses for the game would be more helpful for high-skill bowlers.

In the five weeks following their lesson, the unskilled positive self-monitors had greatly increased their bowling averages by eleven pins per game. This increase in bowling average was one hundred percent better than that of the other low-skilled bowlers in the comparison and control groups. On the other hand, none of the groups of high-skilled bowlers—negative or positive self-monitoring—improved their bowling average. The results led researchers to conclude that "Positive self-monitoring and building on our strengths is best suited to circumstances where we're learning something new, difficult or perceived as difficult."[29]

Job Performance

Philippe Dubreuil from the University of Sherbrooke and his colleagues set out to explore how strengths identification, use, and development can stimulate passion, vitality, and concentration at work, thereby improving work performance. A total of 424 participants, who were members of a human resources association in Canada, were involved in the study. Most participants were females, aged thirty to forty-five years, who had an undergraduate degree.

Participants were asked to complete a number of scales which assessed their strengths-use, level of harmonious passion in their work, subjective vitality, concentration, and work performance (specifically proficiency, adaptiveness, and proactivity).

Results showed that strengths-use was positively associated with work performance. The more that people had opportunities to put their strengths to use at work, the more likely they were to demonstrate work-performance behaviors. Not only were they adequately fulfilling their required tasks, they were also better at adapting to change and acting more proactively in their work environments. The results also suggested that feelings of authenticity, vitality, and concentration play a fundamental role in the explanation of the effects of strengths-use on work performance. It appeared that heightened feelings of energy and aliveness enabled people to work harder and for longer periods of time, as well as to engage in more creative and proactive behaviors, and pay more attention to detail.[30]

Claudia Harzer and Professor Willibald Ruch, of the University of Zurich, have also found replicable associations between character strengths and job performance, specifically the dimensions of task performance, job dedication, interpersonal facilitation, and organizational support. In this study, there were two independent samples, with an average age of forty-one years. Sample 1 consisted of 319 German–speaking employees, and Sample 2 comprised 216 German-speaking participants (108 employees, and 108supervisors) from various occupations such as lawyers, sales, engineers, counselors, teachers, nurses, and office workers.

Participants were asked to complete online surveys including the VIA Survey, the Usefulness of Character Strengths at Work Scale, and questionnaires for each dimension of job performance. After completing the questionnaires, the employees of Sample 2 also had their supervisor fill in ratings. Both employee and supervisor were advised in advance that they'd never see each other's responses.

Across the different occupations studied, the researchers made four key findings:

- Task performance was consistently associated with the character strengths of *perseverance, teamwork, honesty, prudence*, and *self-regulation*. They noted that these findings were anticipated, given that finishing what one starts, doing one's share within a team or organization, not taking undue risks and not saying or doing things that might later be regretted, acting in a sincere way, and taking responsibility for one's actions, play an important role in achieving work outcomes.

- Job dedication was consistently associated with the character strengths of *perseverance, bravery, self-regulation, curiosity*, and *love of learning*. While it might be expected that job dedication would have some conceptual overlap with task performance, the additional strengths of bravery, curiosity, and love of learning refer to behaviors like not shrinking back from challenge or difficulty, taking an interest in an ongoing experience for its own sake, and mastering new skills. Researchers suggested that these character strengths may facilitate extra effort to complete work tasks successfully in spite of difficult conditions and setbacks, the development of one's own knowledge and skills, and taking the initiative to accomplish team objectives.

- Interpersonal facilitation was consistently associated with the character strengths of *teamwork, leadership, fairness*, and *kindness*. Being loyal to the group, encouraging others to get things done, giving everyone a fair chance, and helping others, are behaviors that encourage the motivation of others.

- Organizational support was consistently related to all of the character strengths except six—*forgiveness, humility, appreciation of beauty and excellence, gratitude, humor,* and *spirituality*. This dimension of job performance is related to moral behavior like positively promoting your organization, showing loyalty by staying with it despite hardship, and complying with organizational rules. The numerically highest associations were found with *perseverance, kindness, teamwork,* and *self-regulation*.[31]

Job Meaning and Satisfaction

Professors Hadassah Littman-Ovadia and Michael Steger have found that the recognition and active use of people's character strengths in their work is related to greater work satisfaction, greater wellbeing, and a more meaningful experience in work and life. The researchers explain that "meaning in life" refers to your ability to perceive yourself and the world as worthwhile and valued, identify a unique niche, and establish a valued life purpose. It is positively related to wellbeing, self-realization, fulfillment, job satisfaction, and positive work attitudes.

Their research included three different samples:

- Adolescents volunteering for a medical response organization—the Israeli Red Cross. This comprised of one hundred sophomore, junior, and senior students, and more than half were female. They completed a short version of the VIA Survey, and measures for Strengths Usage, Satisfaction with Volunteer Activities, Wellbeing, and Meaning in Life questionnaires.

- Adults volunteering for a civilian patrol organization—the Civil Guard in Israel. This comprised one hundred adults; sixty-eight percent were men and the mean age was 38.7 years. They completed the same measures as the adolescent volunteers.

- Women working for NA'AMAT, an Israeli nation-wide women's organization that provides daycare, legal advice, labor rights, etc. This comprised 102 female adults, and the mean age was 44.5 years. They completed a short version of the VIA Survey, and measures for Strengths Usage, the Gallup Audit for job satisfaction, Wellbeing, and the Work as Meaning Inventory.

The results found more similarities than differences between the three groups, in that deploying strengths at work appeared to provide key links to satisfaction with voluntary and paid occupational activities among young volunteers, middle-aged volunteers, and adult working women. In particular, the researchers concluded: "Simply endorsing a characteristic as a personal strength was less consistently linked to positive work and wellbeing variables than actually having the chance to deploy those strengths in work activities. Thus, it may not be sufficient to simply think some piece of ourselves is important; it may be vital to enact that piece of ourselves in important domains of life."[32]

In a separate study, Harzer and Ruch also explored how the development of character strengths can impact people's experience of work as a "calling"—or their purpose in life—rather than just a means of financial reward (a job) or advancement (a career). People who experience work as their "calling" have been found in all kinds of jobs, and appear to experience a stronger and more rewarding relationship to their work—including less frequent absent days and higher income.[33] Harzer and Ruch's study consisted of 111 German-speaking adult volunteers across a wide array of occupations. These included medical doctors, lawyers, teachers, mechanics and office workers. More than half of the participants were men, eighty-one percent were highly educated with a master's degree or PhD, and the mean age was 47.21 years.

Participants were asked to rate themselves using the VIA Survey, the Job Satisfaction Questionnaire, the Work Context Questionnaire (which measures pleasure, engagement, and meaning) and the Work-Life Questionnaire (which assesses jobs, careers, and callings"—as defined above). In addition, 111 of their co-workers who knew the participants well, and were therefore able to judge their behavior at work, joined the sample to provide peer ratings. These peer-raters were asked to rate the participants on the Applicability of Character Strengths Rating Scale, which measures the extent that each character strength is applicable at work. Their responses were anonymous, so the self-rater never saw what was said, and they completed the surveys separately from the participants.

The results found associations between the applicability of strengths and the number of positive experiences people were having at work, irrespective of the nature of the strengths. Moreover, the researchers reported it seemed critical to apply at least four signature strengths to create positive experiences at work and a sense of calling.[34]

In another study with 1,111 adults from different occupations, Harzer and Ruch also found that people who used more signature strengths at work were more likely to experience job satisfaction, pleasure, and engagement.[35] Peterson and his colleagues have also found that *curiosity, zest, hope,* gratitude, and *spirituality* are the strengths most often associated with job satisfaction across a variety of occupations.[36] Furthermore, in a study of Israeli college graduates, Littman-Ovadia and Davidovitch found that job satisfaction and wellbeing were correlated with the opportunity for character strength deployment in their work.[37]

Improving the Bottom Line

While leaders often observe that the greatest asset of their organization is its people, in reality, this is only true of employees who are fully engaged in their jobs. Engaged workers stand out from not-engaged and actively disengaged colleagues because of the energy, enthusiasm, and commitment they bring to their work. Willing to go the extra mile because of their emotional connection to the organization, these employees are building new products and services, generating new ideas, creating new customers, and ultimately driving the innovation, growth, and revenue their organizations need—even during difficult times.[38]

Gallup's extensive research shows that engagement is strongly connected to productivity, profitability, and customer satisfaction, which are the outcomes essential to an organization's financial success. Yet their latest findings suggest that seventy percent of American workers and eighty-seven percent of global employees are "not engaged" or "actively disengaged," making them more likely to steal from their companies, negatively influence their coworkers, miss workdays, and drive customers away.[39]

Gallup's research also shows that while keeping employees happy or satisfied is a worthy goal that can help build a more positive workplace and improve employee wellbeing, generous workplace incentives and employee-friendly policies alone are insufficient to create sustainable change, retain top performers, and positively affect the bottom line. In contrast, leaders who focus on their employees' strengths can practically eliminate active disengagement and double the average number of engaged employees across their organization.[40]

The following studies suggest that developing your strengths is not only good for you. It's also good for your team and for your organization. When managers focus on people's strengths, not only do employees feel more engaged, but their levels of productivity, customer satisfaction, and performance also go up. As a result, strengths-led teams achieve higher levels of success.

The Business Case for Improving The Bottom-Line

- **People who use their strengths more are more engaged in their work.**

  Studies have found that employees who have the opportunity to regularly use their strengths at work each day are up to six times more engaged in what they're doing.

- **Managers who focus on people's strengths experience improved team performance and greater success.**

  Studies have found that leaders who focus on the strengths of employees benefit from lower levels of staff turnover, higher levels of productivity, more satisfied customers, and greater profitability.

Employee Engagement

Tom Rath and his colleagues at Gallup conducted a study with a random sample of just over one thousand U.S. employees to determine how much they agreed with two statements:

- My supervisor focuses on my strengths or positive characteristics

- My supervisor focuses on my weaknesses or negative characteristics

Participants who didn't agree with either statement were placed into an "ignored" category.

The results found that one-quarter of American workers fell into the ignored category, and of these, forty percent were actively disengaged. In contrast, managers who focused on their employees' weakness cut active disengagement to twenty-two percent (indicating that even negative attention is better than no attention), while managers who focused on their employees' strengths cut active disengagement to one percent. What's more, sixty-one percent of these employees were engaged—twice as much as the average of U.S. workers nationwide—leading the researchers to conclude: "If every organization in America trained their managers to focus on employees' strengths the U.S. could double the number of engaged employees in the workplace with this one simple shift."[41]

Gallup consultants also completed a study in healthcare organizations in which nine hospitals were assigned various strengths-based interventions over a three-year period, and were then compared to a control group of 151 hospitals. Those hospitals that identified talents and applied strengths-development interventions grew significantly over the three years in terms of employee engagement compared to the control group.[42]

In further research based upon an accumulation of multiple-year employee engagement studies across sixty-five companies, Gallup examined the standard units of growth in employee engagement for four of the companies (in the manufacturing, retail, healthcare, and technology industries) who were given talent identification and strengths-development interventions for two consecutive years. These four companies were compared to the remaining sixty-one different companies, who acted as the controls, using other types of employee-engagement interventions, such as survey feedback and action-planning groups. The researchers report: "From the first to the second year change in the strengths group exceeded that of the control group on employee engagement…and was substantially greater over the first to the third year."[43]

Taking a different approach, Shane Crabb—a chartered business psychologist—conducted a three-year thematic analysis of employee engagement through an extensive review of academic and commercial publications, conferences, presentations, and forums. Results found that focusing on character strengths was among the three most crucial drivers of employee engagement, along with managing emotions and aligning purpose. Specifically, Crabb's results encourage employees to identify, use, and alert others of their signature strengths, as well as to converse with managers about strengths-use opportunities in the organization.[44] Similarly, Minhas's study with university administrators found that work engagement increased when people developed their realized or unrealized strengths.[45]

Team Performance

The Corporate Leadership Council conducted a study of 19, 187 employees from thirty-four organizations across twenty-nine countries. The countries included Latin America, Europe, South Africa, Asia, Australia, and North America, and the organizations spanned seven different industries including retail, manufacturing, technology, healthcare, and banking among others.

It was found that emphasizing strengths had a profound impact on performance. When managers specifically emphasized performance strengths in formal reviews, employees' performance was 36.4 percent higher, and when they emphasized personality strengths, performance was 21.3 percent higher. As a result of positive feedback, these employees were willing to try harder, were more committed to the organization, and felt more comfortable with their work. In contrast, managers who emphasized performance weaknesses saw a 26.8 percent decline in employees' performance, and a 5.5 percent decline was observed for managers who emphasized their employees' personality weaknesses.[46]

Gallup has also found similar results with organizations. For example, in one study of 65,672 employees, turnover rates were almost fifteen percent lower among employees who received feedback on their strengths. While in another study of 530 work units, it was found that units with managers who received strengths feedback—regardless of the type of job they performed—showed over twelve percent higher productivity levels post-intervention relative to units with managers who received no feedback. In another study of 1,874 individual employees—most of them in sales functions—Gallup also found that productivity improved by almost eight percent after a strengths intervention. And in another study of 469 business units within organizations ranging from retail stores to large manufacturing facilities, units with managers who received strengths feedback showed almost nine percent greater profitability.[47]

But it's not just strengths-based feedback that shapes performance. When Gallup studied the responses of 2,000 managers to open-ended questions related to the management of individual talents versus weaknesses, they found that top-performing managers (based on composite performance) were more likely to spend time with high producers, match talents to tasks, and emphasize individual strengths versus seniority in making personnel decisions. As a result, these strengths-based approach managers nearly doubled their likelihood of success, and they were eighty-six percent more likely to achieve above average performance levels than non-strength managers.[48] In fact, in one study of 10,855 work units (308,798 employees) in fifty-one companies, teams who scored above the median on the statement, "At work I have the opportunity to do what I do best every day," had a forty-four percent higher probability of success on customer loyalty and employee retention, and thirty-eight percent higher probability of success on productivity measures. In this case, "success" was defined as exceeding the median performance within their own company across work units. The researchers observed: "Managers who create environments in which employees have a chance to use their talents have more productive work units with less employee turnover."[49]

Mindful Investment

Despite the growing body of evidence suggesting that the identification and development of strengths can be beneficial to the individual, the team, and the organization, Gallup found that only three percent of the thousands of employees who were surveyed for their Strengths Orientation Index can strongly agree on all four of these statements:

- Every week, I set goals and expectations based on my strengths.

- I can name the strengths of five people I work with.

- In the last three months, my supervisor and I have had a meaningful discussion about my strengths.

- My organization is committed to building the strengths of each associate.[50]

Dr. Robert Biswas-Diener and his colleagues noted that while many organizations are still becoming aware of the value of strengths-led approaches, there is currently little agreement on how best to use the theory, research, and assessment tools. They acknowledge that the "identify-and-use" approaches can be an effective and straightforward strategy. However, they argue that the widespread adoption of "strength-development" approaches—which go beyond asking how you might use a strength more, and instead focus on how you might apply the most suitable strength in the right amount, for different situations and outcomes—will lead to better results.[51] Throughout this book, we offer ways to help you, your team, and your organization deliver a more nuanced and theoretically driven strengths-development approach.

The researchers also caution that despite the potential benefits of strength approaches, people can occasionally feel disappointed, disengaged, or otherwise distressed as a result of strengths use. They note: "There is reason to believe that people who adopt a strengths approach to goal pursuit will be more confident and optimistic of success. Thus, when failure occurs, people who more strongly anticipate success may be more disappointed or self-punitive relative to those whose optimism is more cautious."[52]

Emphasizing strengths can make people more psychologically vulnerable to failure, leading to decreased motivation or a perceived threat to a coherent understanding of their own identity. In Chapter 4, we explore the importance of growth mindsets and the focus of strengths-development on learning goals, rather than just outcome goals, to temper this risk. That said, organizations and managers should be mindful that developing strengths might not be appropriate for every employee in every circumstance. And, they should assess and manage potential risks prior to embarking on strength-development approaches.

However, as the evidence in this chapter suggests, for most people, the benefits of being able to develop their strengths leads not just to feeling more engaged, energized, and happy at work—it also improves their physical and mental wellbeing, and their sense of satisfaction with their life. These advantages, in turn, benefit organizations in terms of the potential for higher productivity, lower turnover, and more satisfied customers, which fosters a culture of high-performance.

The good news is, as you'll discover throughout the rest of this book, each of us has strengths that we can use at work every day no matter what our job description says or who we're working for. These strengths do more than just make you unique; they are your—and your organization's—greatest opportunities for growth and success.

PART B
Creating Your Strengths-Development Plan

CHAPTER 3

How Can You Discover Your Strengths?

Everyone has strengths, but do you know how to draw upon those strengths in the workplace? If you're like most of us, you're probably still a little fuzzy on what sets you apart.

You see, while your brain has a built-in negativity bias that makes it easy for you to spot your weaknesses, it generally isn't as well equipped when it comes to identifying your strengths.[1] This is why millions of people over the last decade have turned to *strengths-assessment tools* to find a shared vocabulary that describes what our strengths look like. It's through these measures that people like you have been better able to discover when they're personally at their best.

In this chapter, we'll introduce the most popular strengths-assessment tools that organizations are using today, and help you take these lists of fairly generic strengths descriptions and confidently apply them in your job and within your organization. After all, you don't want to use a character strength like love at work in the wrong way!

Don't worry, this won't hurt a bit. In fact, based on Michelle's experience of helping thousands of people around the world to uncover their strengths, we believe that this will actually be some of the most enjoyable work you will ever undertake.

Choosing Strength-Development Tools

Research suggests that two-thirds of people can't actually name their strengths.[2] Yet, this very simple act of discovering your strengths has been found to give you a short-term boost in productivity.[3] So, what's the best way to go about it?

Some researchers advocate an approach where you simply pay attention to the activities that you most look forward to doing and feel most effective at executing, and that leave you feeling most fulfilled and authentic. These are the moments where you feel alive, fully engaged, and completely immersed in an activity. For example, time flies by for Michelle at work when she's creating videos to teach others how to flourish; and Erin feels fully engaged when she's able to structure and organize information in a meaningful way to aid her own and others' learning. Researchers argue that one way to surface your strengths is to note down your experiences of these occurrences over a week or more and look for the common themes.[4]

Other researchers recommend using an Individual Strengths Assessment with a strengths coach who can guide you through a series of questions to help you discover when you're at your best. The questions may include:

- What makes a really good day for you?
- What gives you the greatest sense of being authentic and who you really are?
- What are the most energizing things you do?
- What are you most looking forward to in the future?
- Thinking about your next week, what will you be doing when you're at your best?[5]

You will find strengths coaches, through a simple Google search, who can guide you through this approach.

Based on Michelle's experience, we believe that it is often most helpful to use a tested measurement tool to guide you through answering a series of well-researched questions from which your unique strengths can be identified. The three most popular tools in the world at present are the *Gallup StrengthsFinder*, the *Values in Action (VIA) Survey*, and *Realise2*. So which one might be right for you?

StrengthsFinder 2.0

While working for the Gallup Research organization in the mid-1990s, Clifton and his grandson, Tom Rath, teamed up to create a systematic approach for assessing people's strengths in the workplace. Drawing on Clifton's decades of research of employees across a range of professions, organizations, and roles, they started with six hundred questions that seemed to have some relevance to job success. Slowly they narrowed these six hundred questions down to a list of 187. Looking at the answers to each question, they began searching for clusters of *talents* and kept refining their list until each talent was distinct and could be named in one word.[6]

After testing early versions of this list of talents on hundreds of subjects with the help of psychology professors at Harvard and UCLA, Clifton and Rath ended up with thirty-four patterns of talent—or "themes" of talent as they later called them—capturing everything from connectedness to responsibility, empathy, discipline, and communication. Of course, it's impossible to narrow the breadth of human idiosyncrasy in any one list, but the final thirty-four were found to be the most prevalent examples of human talent and, in their many combinations, appeared the best way to capture the broadest range of excellent performance.[7]

These thirty-four themes of talent were used as the foundation for *StrengthsFinder*—an online assessment to identify areas where people had the greatest potential for building on their strengths.[8] To complete the survey, visit http://www.strengthstest.com. Here you will purchase an access code and then answer 180 paired statements—such as, "I read instructions carefully", and "I like to jump right into things"—by selecting the response that most accurately describes you within twenty seconds. The time limit is designed to mirror the speed of real-life decision-making, so you have enough time to read and comprehend both statements, but not enough time to allow your intellect to affect your choice.[9] Scores are then assigned to your answers, enabling your strengths to be ranked from highest to lowest across the thirty-four different themes of talent.

Your final results don't attempt to define you completely or label you as one type or another, or "strong here" and "weak there." Rather, the results have been designed to reveal your five dominant themes of talent, known as your "signature themes." Researchers believe the "signature themes" represent your greatest potential for developing your strengths and the best pathways to help you achieve consistent, near-perfect performances that are both excellent and fulfilling.[10]

It's important to note that these themes of talent may not be strengths . . . yet. Each theme is a recurring pattern of thought, feeling, or behavior— the promise of a strength that can be built upon with the investment of knowledge and skills.

It's also worth remembering that if you don't like one of your talent themes, researchers believe that these themes will prove resistant to change no matter how much you might yearn to transform yourself. However, bear in mind that you can acquire new knowledge and skills to amplify your talents, and these new acquisitions may well lead you into exciting new arenas.[11]

So what does this mean for your weaknesses? Unfortunately, we each have countless areas where we lack proficiency, but Clifton recommends we ignore these weaknesses, as they are simply not worth bothering about. Why? Because he believes the only weaknesses that matter are those that get in the way of excellent performance. As a result, he suggests weaknesses are simply managed around.[12]

For example, if you're lacking in a talent theme such as *communication*, which might have been harmless in your previous role as a research law clerk, it's likely to become a bigger weakness the moment you decide to become a trial lawyer and are required to spend more of your time communicating your ideas to others. If this is truly a lack of talent—rather than just a lack of knowledge or skills—then creative ways to manage around its absence might include:

- Designing a support system or crutch to make it a little easier;
- Using a stronger talent to overwhelm your short comings;
- Partnering with a colleague who does have this talent; or
- No longer trying to perform this behavior and seeing if anyone really cares when it comes to your work.

In 2009, Gallup conducted further research with thousands of executive teams and discovered that the thirty-four themes could also be naturally clustered under four distinct domains of leadership: *executing, influencing, relationship building,* and *strategic thinking.* Although the categories appear to be quite general, these broad domains have been found to offer a practical lens for looking at the composition of a team. Research suggests that the strongest teams have a diversity of talents across each of these domains. Although individuals need not be well-rounded, it appears that teams should be.[13]

The Four Domains of Leadership Strength

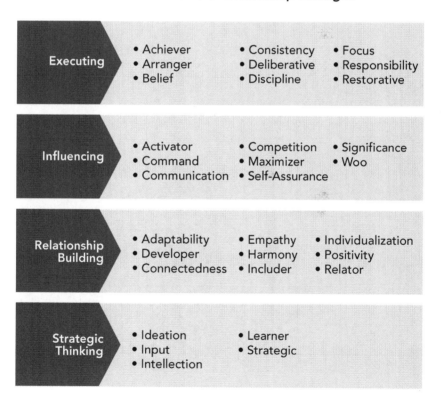

Executing
- Achiever
- Arranger
- Belief
- Consistency
- Deliberative
- Discipline
- Focus
- Responsibility
- Restorative

Influencing
- Activator
- Command
- Communication
- Competition
- Maximizer
- Self-Assurance
- Significance
- Woo

Relationship Building
- Adaptability
- Developer
- Connectedness
- Empathy
- Harmony
- Includer
- Individualization
- Positivity
- Relator

Strategic Thinking
- Ideation
- Input
- Intellection
- Learner
- Strategic

StrengthsFinder is used by a growing number of workplaces and has been completed by more than nine million people to date. Many users find it to be a helpful tool for introducing a vocabulary of strengths into their organization and discovering the talents of their employees. However, some researchers remain skeptical about the efficacy of the assessment. Gallup-employed scientists remain the only evaluators of the measures on which it is founded.[14]

Based on Michelle's experience, we believe that this tool can be a helpful way to identify what you like to do in your job—those things you want to be paid and recognized for. If you can't list your top five talents, we recommend completing this tool as a helpful starting place.

Values in Action (VIA) Survey

In 1999, Dr. Neal Mayerson, President of The Mayerson Foundation, asked Seligman how he could support research exploring positive psychology's hope of helping people to realize their full potential and live "the good life." They quickly discovered that the challenge with devising an intervention to bring out the best in people was finding a way to measure what was "good" about a person.

Having had a front-row seat when the decision was made by psychologists to define all that goes wrong with people (leading to the creation of DSM-III, the third revision of the diagnostic and statistical manual of mental disorders), Seligman realized that for positive psychology to succeed, there needed to be an equivalent classification system for all that goes right with people. With Mayerson's sponsorship, the VIA Institute was created.

Peterson took the helm as the director of virtues, and over three years he led fifty-three social scientists from around the world in gathering examples—and the means to measure and improve them—that represented humanity at its best from history, philosophy, religion, psychology, and modern culture. After leaving no stone unturned in assembling an exhaustive list of these *character strengths*, the final list was narrowed by combining redundancies and applying criteria like:

- **Ubiquitous**—the character strength is valued across time and culture.

- **Fulfilling**—the character strength contributes to individual fulfillment, satisfaction, and happiness.

- **Morally valued**—the character strength is valued in its own right and not for tangible outcomes.

- **Trait-like**—the character strength differs between individuals with demonstrable generality and stability across time and context.

- **Does not diminish others**—the character strength doesn't harm others, but rather uplifts and inspires them when it's seen in action.

- **Can be selectively absent**—the character strength is missing altogether in some people.

- **Measurable**—patterns of particular character strengths can be identified in people's behaviors, thoughts, and feelings.

On this last point, it is worth noting that methods for reliably assessing humility, bravery, and modesty are still in progress.[15]

From this research emerged the VIA Classification, or as Seligman likes to call it, "the manual of the sanities," which contains twenty-four character strengths organized under six core virtues: *wisdom and knowledge, courage, humanity, justice, temperance,* and *transcendence.*

The Six Virtue Clusters of Character Strengths

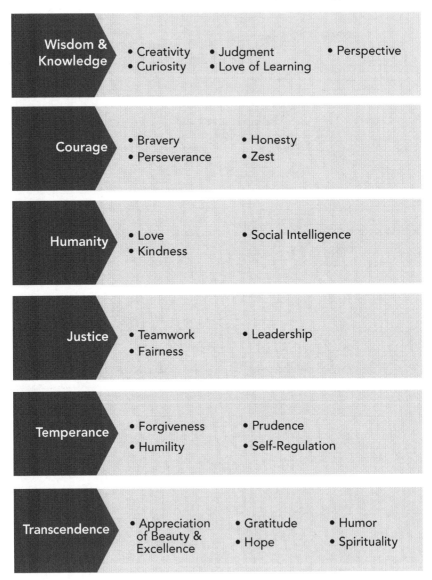

Wisdom & Knowledge
- Creativity
- Curiosity
- Judgment
- Love of Learning
- Perspective

Courage
- Bravery
- Perseverance
- Honesty
- Zest

Humanity
- Love
- Kindness
- Social Intelligence

Justice
- Teamwork
- Fairness
- Leadership

Temperance
- Forgiveness
- Humility
- Prudence
- Self-Regulation

Transcendence
- Appreciation of Beauty & Excellence
- Gratitude
- Hope
- Humor
- Spirituality

Peterson rightly noted upon its release that he expected future groupings of the character strengths to be revised, expanded, or contracted as more is learned from this taxonomy. For example, some researchers have already suggested that the twenty-four character strengths are more accurately classified under three or four categories—such as intellectual strengths, interpersonal strengths, and temperance strengths—as opposed to the six initially proposed virtue clusters.[16]

Based upon these twenty-four character strengths, the *VIA Survey* can be completed for free at www.viainstitute.org in about ten minutes. You'll answer 120 statements using a five-point scale (from "very much like me" to "very much unlike me"). For example, statements include, "I find the world a very interesting place," which gauges *curiosity*, or "I always let bygones be bygones," which gauges *forgiveness*. Overall, a higher score for particular statements indicates that you more strongly identify with a particular character strength.

At the completion of the survey, your answers are sorted according to their scores; creating an ordered list from highest to lowest to indicate how these twenty-four character strengths appear within you currently. Researchers encourage you to pay particular attention to your top four to six strengths—these are your "signature strengths." Studies have found that people who use four or more of their signature strengths have more positive work experiences than those who use less than four.[17]

It's important to be aware that due to the way the VIA Survey scores your answers, if you end up with a tie between, say, your fifth and sixth strength, then it will simply sort them alphabetically. If your sixth and seventh strength are running in alphabetical order, we recommend including these in your signature strengths if they feel just as authentic and invigorating for you as those higher on your results.

You can see the exact scores for each of your strengths by purchasing an additional report on the VIA website. It will also help you to categorize your strengths by the six virtue groups, and you'll be able to use the report to gain more insight into what each strength means and how it can be applied.

If you find yourself heading straight down the list to see what your twenty-fourth strength is, then don't despair. This is just your negativity bias at work. Researchers are quick to point out that each of the character strengths is a strength in its own right because it is morally valued. It remains an example of human life at its best. This means that your twenty-fourth character strength is not a weakness per se. Rather, it's just that your infrequent use of that character strength means you have less ability to apply it than your top strengths.[18]

The most important thing is how you feel about your results, rather than what your actual results are. Most people tend to have one of three responses:

- **"Yes, that's me, and I feel proud of these results."** If this is your response, the challenge then becomes finding ways to use these strengths at work consistently.

- **"Why is that strength down there?"** If this is your response, the challenge then becomes finding ways to put more energy into the strengths you value but haven't been using lately. Remember, each of your character strengths is buildable.

- **"That doesn't look anything like me."** If this is your response, then share your results with colleagues, friends, or family who know you well. Ask them what they think your top strengths are, and then trust their guidance and your own experiences to prioritize the strengths you want to be using more at work.

As Peterson once told Michelle, "It's a tool not a magical oracle. It doesn't know anything you probably don't already know about yourself."

It also helps to remember that character strengths are within us, but we live within settings, and so we need to manage the two elements together. For example, a group of New Yorkers completed the VIA Survey not long before 9/11. For this group, *bravery* was found to be one of the middle strengths for most participants. After the tragic events that unfolded in New York, the same group was asked to complete the survey once again, and, not surprisingly given the situation they found themselves in, *bravery* was now one of the top strengths for almost every participant.[19]

Character strengths are shaped by context, meaning that they don't operate in isolation from the settings you find yourself in. This means that it's worth retaking the survey annually or whenever big shifts are going on in your life—for example, if you're changing jobs, moving to a new city, or there's a new arrival in your family. When you do this year after year, you'll find that many of your character strengths remain fairly consistent, but several move around depending on your current context and the strengths you're drawing on most in these situations.

The VIA Survey is used by a growing number of workplaces, schools, and communities, and has been completed by more than 2.6 million people in 190 different countries to date. Like StrengthsFinder, many users find it to be a helpful tool to build a vocabulary of strengths in their organization and discover the things that intrinsically motivate them to act. Unlike StrengthsFinder, the VIA Survey is peer-reviewed with the findings of independent researchers published in scientific journals in terms of its reliability and validity. Although there are always concerns that people paint a more favorable picture of themselves in self-reported subjective-ranking tools, studies have found that results are typically endorsed by the friends and family members of those who complete the test.[20]

Based on Michelle's experience, we believe that the VIA Survey is an incredibly helpful way to identify how you like to work in your job—those things you value about what you do each day. If you can't list your top five character strengths, we recommend completing this tool as the best starting place. And, to help you understand what each of the character strengths listed on your survey results actually mean, you can refer to the Appendix at the back of this book to find a helpful definition of each of them.

Realise2

In 2009, based on extensive research with individuals and organizations, Dr. Alex Linley and his colleagues at The Center for Applied Positive Psychology (CAPP) decided it was time for a second-generation strengths-development and assessment tool. They believed that while the Gallup StrengthsFinder and the VIA Survey were helpful in establishing shared vocabularies around strengths, additional benefits could be gained by giving people more insight into how to apply their strengths.

CAPP defines a strength as, "the things that we are good at and that give us energy when we are using them." Based on this description, there are three core parts to a strength: performance (how good we are at doing something); energy (how much energy we get from doing it); and use (how often we get to do it). CAPP differentiates a strength from:

- **Learned behaviors**—which you can perform well but don't actually enjoy doing. These behaviors drain you, leaving you feeling disengaged and at risk of burn out.

- **Weaknesses**—which you perform poorly and find de-energizing. They leave you feeling bad and lacking in motivation.

- **Unrealized Strengths**—which you can perform well, find energizing, but don't do very much of. This is where you have the greatest opportunity for development and growth.

From these definitions, *Realise2* was created to help you discover your strengths and to help you realize the inherent potential within them to facilitate your individual and organizational development. Based on years of research, CAPP collated their observations regarding strengths and high performance and refined the descriptions and definitions into particular attributes. Having examined over one hundred different strengths, they narrowed this down to sixty strengths that are used as the basis for Realise2. CAPP believes these sixty strengths are the broadest and most representative basis for assessing strengths in the general population.[21]

They also clustered the strengths on a conceptual basis into "strengths families" to capture the broad range of human activity and interaction. These include:

The Five Strengths Families

Strengths of Being			
• Authenticity	• Humility	• Pride	
• Centered	• Legacy	• Self-awareness	
• Courage	• Mission	• Service	
• Curiosity	• Moral Compass	• Unconditionality	
• Gratitude	• Personal Responsibility		

Strengths of Communicating			
• Counterpoint	• Feedback	• Listener	• Scribe
• Explainer	• Humor	• Narrator	• Spotlight

Strengths of Motivating			
• Action	• Change Agent	• Efficacy	• Persistence
• Adventure	• Competitive	• Growth	• Resilience
• Bounce-back	• Drive	• Improver	• Work Ethic
• Catalyst			

Strengths of Relating			
• Compassion	• Enabler	• Persuasion	
• Connector	• Equality	• Rapport Builder	
• Emotional Awareness	• Esteem Builder	• Relationship	
• Empathic Connection	• Personalization	Deepener	

Strengths of Thinking				
• Adherence	• Innovation	• Planful	• Strategic	
• Creativity	• Judgment	• Prevention	• Awareness	
• Detail	• Optimism	• Reconfiguration	• Time Optimizer	
• Incubator	• Order	• Resolver		

71

To complete the survey, visit https://realise2.cappeu.com, where you will purchase a code to assess your strengths. The survey uses a seven-point scale for three different axes: how energizing you find an activity (energy), how good you are at the activity (performance), and how often you actually do the activity (use). Rather than simply focusing on your top strengths, it provides you with a report that details your *realized strengths*, your *unrealized strengths*, your *learned behaviors*, and your *weaknesses*, with the goal being to give you a more holistic picture of who you are, why you do what you do, and the areas where you will shine and where you will struggle.

To help you achieve optimal performance through making the most of your strengths, moderating your learned behaviors, and minimizing your weaknesses, Realise2 recommends the following applications (known as the 4M model):

- **Minimize Weaknesses to make them Irrelevant:** CAPP believes that a weakness is a weakness and that it's best to accept this and focus your development attention elsewhere. To minimize your weaknesses, try to reshape what you do, use your strengths to compensate, find a complementary partner, or adopt ways to work as a team so that each person can draw on their strengths. If none of these approaches are possible, it is recommended that you undertake training to gain a basic level of competence.

- **Moderate Learned Behaviors for Sustainable Performance:** Use learned behaviors as appropriate and as needed, while recognizing that they won't ever be the road to sustainable high performance. To moderate your learned behaviors, try to stop doing them, refocus your role, organize tasks and activities into a "strengths sandwich" to balance energizing and draining activities, look for complimentary partners, and adopt strength-based team working.

- **Marshal Realized Strengths for Optimal Performance:** Get the best from your strengths by making them productive. Make sure you understand your strengths, connect your strengths to the goals you want to achieve, combine multiple strengths together to amplify your effect, be mindful not to overplay your strengths, and monitor and refine your application of strengths in different situations.

- **Maximize Unrealized Strengths for Growth and Development:** If you want to turbo-charge your growth and development, focus on your unrealized strengths. Look for opportunities to use these strengths more frequently, be sure to practice them, develop and hone your applications, gradually expand, and then evaluate how you're deploying these strengths and the results you're achieving.[22] For example, when Michelle was trying to maximize her unrealized strength of humor, she tried to find one opportunity each day to share a story that lightened the mood and made others laugh.

Like the VIA character strengths, the creators of Realise2 believe that as people move into different contexts, some strengths will advance to the foreground and others will recede to the background. Thus, they recommend retaking the survey at regular intervals to check in on how your strengths, particularly your realized and unrealized strengths, may be shifting.

Realise2 is also used by a growing number of workplaces and has been completed by more than seventy thousand people to date.[23] It is a more sophisticated tool in terms of interpreting the data it provides, so many users find it helps to have an accredited practitioner to debrief their results. While CAPP report extensive evidence for the reliability and validity of Realise2 and provide a detailed technical manual with research to date, peer-reviewed studies by independent researchers for scientific journals have not been completed on this tool.

In Michelle's experience, while the more dynamic lens through which this tool helps you to understand your strengths can be valuable, people find Realise2 more complex to apply than StrengthsFinder or the VIA Survey. This is because there are more strengths to learn and remember, and at times, the results appear force-fitted into categories like "weaknesses" simply because scores were high on all other dimensions. However, if you'd like a more nuanced understanding of your strengths, then this tool certainly offers additional depth.

Case In Point

By Michelle McQuaid

When I work with organizations to help people discover their strengths, the first question is always the same: "What's the best way to get started?" I believe a good assessment tool is like a good woodworking tool—it must be designed to fit the job being done. To determine which of the strengths discovery tools best suits you or your organization, you must be clear on the questions you want answered and on how the results can be used to deliver desired business outcomes.

For most of the organizations I work with—whether it's a bank, a technology company, a pharmaceutical leader, a government department, or a school—I've found the VIA Survey coupled with a review of how you're already developing your strengths at work is generally the best way to get started. Not only is the VIA Survey tool free (which means it meets anyone's budget), but there are five key learnings that make it a preferred tool for discovering strengths in organizations.

- **New discoveries tend to drive action**. It's common for people who have completed a strength-discovery tool to encounter an "aha" moment where they realize their job is not well matched to their strengths and recognize what it is costing them professionally and personally. But what happens next? By focusing on "how" we like to work and the experiences we want, the VIA Survey offers plenty of immediate, practical ways to apply our strengths, no matter "what" we're required to do in our jobs. I've found that it's a graceful way to create evolutions, rather than revolutions, in people's careers.

- **The possibility of change opens us to hope.** Reducing people's identities to a number, a series of letters, or a fixed set of talents denies the dynamic complexity that constitutes human life. As scientists continue to unravel the mysteries of the brain, it seems premature to believe the sum of who we are can be put in a box and labeled for eternity. By recognizing that our strengths are buildable and changeable in different contexts, the VIA Survey provides a moment-in-time snapshot of who we are at our best without limiting our capacity for change and growth. I've found it sparks hope about the kind of people we can become.

- **Understanding motivation improves engagement.** You only have to look at the declining levels of employee engagement in most organizations to see that many leaders struggle to understand how to motivate themselves and their people. By shedding light on our intrinsic motivators, the VIA Survey makes it easier to identify the opportunities we value at work even if we're not paid or recognized for them. I've found it quickly engages untapped potential.

- **Simplicity makes sharing easy.** Most people struggle to identify strengths in themselves and others because they lack a common vocabulary to describe what they're seeing. By offering a smaller number of culturally universal strengths, the VIA Survey helps create a shared language that is readily understood. I've found that people are much more likely to remember, value, and appreciate these strengths in action for themselves and each other.

- **Depth of application doesn't require complexity.** After discovering their strengths, most people are left wondering what to do next. By drawing on your character strengths to envision your future, create development plans, and build small daily habits, the VIA Survey provides plenty of insight into how to structure your work in ways that are engaging, energizing, and enjoyable without rigidly directing you to certain behaviors. I've found it provides enough depth to create meaningful and robust individual development plans and effectively manage the people processes for large organizations.

As their strengths-development approach becomes established, I will sometimes suggest that an organization adds more tools, such as StrengthsFinder or Realise2, to aid their strengths discoveries. Using these tools in combination with the VIA Survey can yield new levels of insight for those who thrive on more detail and complexity.

For most organizations though, I find the VIA Survey is more than enough to meet their needs. After all, discovering your strengths is just one part of the puzzle—developing them each day is where the real work begins.

*Transparency note: Michelle's work with organizations using the VIA Survey has become so extensive that the VIA Institute has engaged her to consult in the creation of workplace-training materials from time to time. However, long before this relationship and in between consulting periods, Michelle continues to recommend starting with the VIA Survey because of the reasons noted above.

Finding Your Strengths in the Real World

Regardless of which assessment tool you choose to use, a generic list of your strengths is of limited value unless you can also identify how they can be effectively applied in your role and in your organization. Applying a talent like *woo* (your ability to win others over), a character strength like *love* (your desire to develop and foster strong relationships with others), or a realized strength like *resolver* (your enjoyment of solving problems) could look very different depending on who you work for and the job you're expected to do.

The most recent research has helped us understand that the real power of discovering your strengths comes from turning theory into practice by finding what scientists call the *"golden mean"* of your strengths: not too little, not too much, but just the right strength, in just the right amount, for just the right situation. By helping you understand the complex web of situational, social, and psychological factors, this approach enables you to address a range of behaviors from unrealized potential to optimal outcomes.[24]

Finding the golden mean of your strengths means knowing at work when you're:

- **At your best**: These are the "Goldilocks moments" when you feel your strengths are "just right"—when you're engaged, energized and enjoying what you're doing at work. They are the high-point moments in your career. They're memorable because you couldn't wait to get into the office, the day just flew by, and when you walked out of the office at the end of the day you felt proud and satisfied about your efforts.

- **Underplaying your strengths**: These are the times when your lack of confidence—due to blindness about your strengths or uncertainty around how to apply them in a valuable way—is holding you back, dimming you down, or disengaging you for fear of ridicule or failure. The challenge is that even when we know our strengths, many of us feel that we don't have permission to use them at work because they're not listed in our job description or we don't know if they'll be appreciated in our work culture.

  For example, women often tell us they don't feel like they can use the character strength of *love* at work for fear they'll be seen as "too nice" or "too soft" in more male-dominated environments. Yet thriving at work is less about how we perform the assigned tasks and more about being able to express who we are through the work that we do so it feels engaging and meaningful. Finding valued ways to stop underplaying your strengths is an essential part of balancing your strengths and ensuring your sustainable success at work.

- **Overplaying your strengths:** These are the times at work when even though everything should be going well because you have the opportunity to do what you do best, things aren't quite coming together. It may be that you're so energized by the chance to use your strengths that you've taken them too far and are creating havoc or burning yourself out. Or, it could be that the context you're currently in doesn't require that particular strength right now. Although Clifton may not entirely concur, other researchers do agree that every strength has what's called a "shadow side." This refers to those times where your strength becomes a derailer rather than an enabler.[25]

Examples of shadow sides include:

- People with the character strength of *honesty* can be too blunt.

- People with the character strength of *humor* are prone to making a joke at the wrong time.

- People with the character strength of *perseverance* can become consumed by finishing a task.

- People with the character strengths of *kindness* and *love* tend to give and give and give to everybody else until there's nothing left for themselves, leaving them rundown and exhausted.

Based on Michelle's experience, we believe that if you scratch below the surface of most performance feedback regarding your "weaknesses" at work, chances are you'll find a strength that's being overplayed. When you think about the neurological challenges of improving a strength versus fixing a weakness, wouldn't you rather explore ways to simply dial some of your strengths back or fine-tune their application? Most people find this to be much easier and more appealing. For a little extra help as you go, take a look at the Appendix at the back of this book for examples of shadow sides for each character strength, and suggestions for overcoming them.

The good news is that you already have an untapped reservoir of clear examples of your own strengths in action to guide you in finding your golden mean. Where? Just use the play sheet at the end of this chapter to think back on some of the different experiences you've already had in your career. In the next chapter, we'll help you discover the possibilities this can open up for the work that you're already doing and the work you want to do in the future.

Case In Point

By Michelle McQuaid

The first time I discovered my strengths using the VIA Survey was while I was obtaining my masters in applied positive psychology, where I had the good fortune to be taught by the late Professor Chris Peterson. I remember looking at my results and feeling quite surprised that character strengths like zest, curiosity, creativity, hope, and gratitude encapsulated me at my best. I had just never thought of myself in this light.

Yet, when I reflected on my best moments at work, like creating a global brand campaign to pilot in one country before rolling it out around the world, it was clear that my strengths of creativity and curiosity were consistently present. I've always thought of myself as a reasonably creative person, but I never would have described myself as curious before completing the survey. As I reflected on more of my high-point moments at work, however, it became evident that curiosity was everywhere. I had spent most of my career completely blind to this strength, but with my eyes now wide open, I quickly found new levels of success and fulfillment in my work by mindfully embracing this strength in different situations.

When I reflected on some of the opportunities I had missed at work because I hesitated or held myself back—like building change champion networks to execute the strategies I was responsible for delivering—it was clear I was underplaying my strengths of *hope* and *gratitude*. As a natural introvert, I'd much rather think about ideas than talk about ideas with people, but to execute a global brand campaign, you need to do both with a reasonable level of proficiency. To make the people-side of my work more engaging, energizing, and enjoyable, I started experimenting with my strength of *hope* to unite our teams around the world behind a common goal, as well as my strength of *gratitude* to take the time to respect, value, and appreciate others for all they offered. In a matter of months, we'd built a global network that was instrumental in delivering results we'd never been able to achieve previously, and we had a lot of fun in the process.

When I reflected on some of the moments at work when, despite my best efforts, what I'd done hadn't really been appreciated—like trying to create a new set of brand values—there was one consistent piece of developmental feedback that kept ringing in my ears from bosses over the years: "Slow down a bit so others can catch up." To be honest, I struggled to understand this counsel when they were patting me on the back for all that I was getting done, and then smacking me in the head for going too fast. Perhaps, more importantly, I had no idea how to slow down. The very idea ran contrary to the way I was motivated to live my life.

When I discovered that *zest*—energy and vitality—was my top character strength, this feedback finally made sense. When overplayed, my strength of *zest* had me running off at one hundred miles an hour on a new project—creating ideas, setting timelines, and executing plans—only to realize later that most of my team and stakeholders were still milling around the starting line wondering when the starter's gun was fired.

By better understanding my strength of zest, I was able to become more proficient in ways to apply it well, use it more frequently in the right situations, and regulate it in the moments when a slower approach was needed. Instead of leaving people behind, I was able to bring them with me on the journey. As a result, during future performance reviews, my "weakness" of going too fast was never mentioned again and instead I was commended for my ability to take teams with me.

Finding the golden mean of my strengths is a constant work in progress. As I've become more mindful of dialing up and dialing down my strengths in different situations, particularly when fear holds me back or I'm frustrated and exhausted, I've relished having the choices and tools to respond in ways that allow me to show up, shine, and succeed in ways I never would have imagined.

Discover Your Strengths Play Sheet

1. Choose the assessment tool that most suits your needs. We recommend starting with the free VIA Survey (www.viainstitute.org) to discover *how* you like to work and the experiences that bring out your best. If you'd like to discover more about *what* you like to do at work and the outcomes you like to achieve—and you're happy to pay a small fee—try StrengthsFinder (http://www.strengthstest.com). If you'd like to understand more about what energizes you, boosts your performance, and you're happy to pay a small fee, then Realise2 (https://realise2.cappeu.com) might be for you.

2. When you review your results, tune in to how you're feeling about them.

    *   Do you feel satisfied with the picture your results are painting? If yes, your challenge will be finding ways to apply your strengths more consistently at work.

    *   Are you wondering why certain strengths are rated differently than you expected? If yes, your challenge will be finding ways to use the strengths you value but may not be practicing regularly at work.

    *   Do the strengths not feel at all like you? If yes, check in with colleagues, friends, or family who know you well and ask where they would rate your strengths. Use their feedback to determine the most accurate ratings for you.

3. Put your results into context by thinking back on how you've used, or not used, these strengths at work to understand what they look like in your role and in your organization. These may be big moments, such as acting in a particular role or on a specific project, or completing a task under a certain boss. They may be much smaller moments like one conversation with a client, a team meeting you loved, or an exciting learning opportunity. They may be quite recent moments or ones that occurred some time ago.

Discover Your Strengths Play Sheet (continued)

- Think back on a high-point moment—a time that is memorable and stands out when you've felt really engaged, energized, and enjoying what you were doing at work. What exactly was happening in this moment? What were you doing? How did you feel? What makes this moment so memorable? And, most importantly, which of your top strengths were you using (there may be more than one strength in play)?

If you're struggling to spot your strengths, try sharing the story and your survey results with someone else. Ask them which of your strengths they think were used.

- Think back on a time when you missed an opportunity at work because you lacked confidence, feared failure, or you didn't want to stand out from your peers. What exactly was happening in this moment? What were you working on? How did it feel to hold yourself back? What might it have cost you or your team? And, most importantly, which of your top five character strengths or talents could you have called upon to help you show up and shine in this situation?

    If you're struggling to find the strengths you might be underplaying, share your survey results with someone who knows you and your work well. Ask if there are particular strengths they think will be helpful for you to dial-up.

- Finally, think back on a time when despite putting in your best efforts things seemed to have misfired, people didn't appreciate what you were doing, and you may have almost burned yourself out. What *exactly* was happening in this moment? How did it feel to be working so hard and yet still be unable to deliver the results you wanted to or be appreciated for your efforts? What did this cost you personally and

Discover Your Strengths Play Sheet (continued)

professionally? And which of your strengths were you overplaying in this situation that, if dialed back a little, could have helped you get a better outcome?

If you're struggling to find the strengths you might be overplaying, ask someone who knows you well to look at your survey results and any development feedback—formal or informal—you've been given in the past to see if there are particular strengths you might have a tendency to overplay in your worst moments.

Try to find a couple of examples for each of these points if you can. If you're struggling for examples, look back on past feedback you've had about your work performance—good and bad—and see if you can spot the strengths in play. Or ask people who have worked with you and know you well if they can help with examples of where your strengths are underplayed, overplayed, and just right.

Then, be alert over the coming week. You may even want to keep a journal of your best and worst moments at work. Try to note each time what you're doing, how you're feeling, and whether you're underplaying, overplaying, or have found the golden mean of particular strengths or strength constellations.

The more examples you can gather, the easier it will be to take the next step of envisioning what a strengths-balanced future could look like at work.

CHAPTER 4

How Can You Dream of a Strengths-Fueled Future?

Now that you've discovered your strengths and what they currently look like in your real world, it's time to make some space to imagine what might be possible if you found the golden mean of your strengths more often at work. After all, it's almost impossible to reach the destination you're longing for if you don't have some idea of what it actually looks like.

This isn't an exercise in wishing. Rather, we'll introduce you to the growing body of evidence that demonstrates how positive images of the future neurologically pull us forward by prompting us to take action in the present. As always, our goal is to harness the way our brain is naturally wired to make it easier, more engaging, and more effective to achieve the outcomes you want.

In this chapter, we'll share the scientific formula for creating more golden-mean moments with your strengths, explore the purpose for which you want to apply your strengths more effectively, and understand what a strengths-fueled future might look like in your work. There may be places where this chapter feels a little daunting, especially if you haven't spent much time thinking about what you want for your work and for your life. We urge you to stick with it and complete the provided play sheets, because this step enables you to truly create the lasting changes you're craving.

Developing Your Golden Mean

Consistently hitting the golden mean of your strengths—where you're using them in ways that are just right for the situation and the outcomes you want—lies in the art of what psychologists call *"flow."* Flow is the feeling you have when time stops and you lose all self-consciousness because you're fully absorbed in what you're doing. Awareness and action are merged, so you may not be thinking or feeling anything, and yet you're learning, growing, improving, and advancing so that you feel more capable, confident, and satisfied afterwards. It is engagement in the fullest sense, which allows you to perform at your best and experience great pleasure from what you're doing.[1]

The good news is that we all experience flow in our lives from time to time. You might describe it as "being in the zone" or "feeling one with the music." Unfortunately, most of us are completely unaware of what happens to create these moments, which makes it difficult for us to spend more time in them.

Renowned professor Mihaly Csikszentmihalyi discovered the concept of flow. He explains that this state occurs when you have a clear goal that balances your strengths with the complexity of the task at hand; when you receive regular feedback on how you're going; and when you feel a sense of autonomy.[2]

For example, imagine your goal was to complete a detailed piece of research for your work, and the complexity of the task was balanced with your strength of curiosity. You had some choice on how you went about the task, and you were given feedback on the insights you were gathering. It is highly likely that you'd find yourself in a state of flow as you completed this project. The golden mean of your curiosity—the right strength, at the right time, for the right outcome—is perfectly matched to the situation.

However, if your goal was to complete a detailed piece of research, but you found the complexity of the task was far too simple for your strength of curiosity, then rather than finding yourself in a state of flow, you're more likely to experience a state of boredom. In Michelle's experience, this kind of situation can lead to overplaying your strength by failing to meet the needs of your stakeholders in terms of volume, complexity, or application of the report you're creating. To ensure your efforts are valued, try to get your stakeholders to agree to a scope of work you'll find more interesting. Challenge yourself to develop lesser strengths as you complete the task, or try to balance it with other work or a passion project that makes better use of your strengths.

On the other hand, if your goal was to complete a detailed piece of research, but you found the complexity of the task was far more difficult than your strength of curiosity could currently support, then rather than finding yourself in a state of flow, you're more likely to experience a state of anxiety. This kind of situation can lead you to hesitate due to a lack of confidence, as well as to underplay your strengths. Instead of procrastinating or putting off whatever you've been asked to do in this situation, try to seek out other people who might complement your strength and make the task easier. Ask for coaching or training support to help you develop the strength further, or simply give yourself permission to just keep using the strength to the best of your ability with the understanding that you're working toward mastery.

Why bother? Studies have found that the state of flow comes with a host of benefits. In these moments, you feel more involved in your life rather than isolated from it. You enjoy activities far more, rather than feeling bored. You have a stronger sense of control, rather than feelings of helplessness that can overwhelm you from time to time. And you enjoy a stronger sense of self, have more self-belief, and have a higher level of confidence in what you're actually capable of doing.[3]

Unfortunately, there are two beliefs many of us hold about our work that makes accessing the state of flow more difficult than it needs to be.

First, despite all the neurological evidence to the contrary, sixty-one percent of us still think we grow the most in our areas of weakness.[4] While studies suggest that you can take a weakness and turn it into a strength, it's estimated that this would require around eight to ten thousand hours of deliberate practice.[5] This is why researchers believe that you learn the most, grow the most, and develop the most in your areas of greatest strength.[6] To access a state of flow, you have to believe in the value of developing your strengths and mindfully set about this practice each day.

Secondly, research suggests that ninety-one percent of us believe that a good team member does whatever it takes to help the team.[7] After all, there's no "I" in team, right? The truth is, high-performing teams identify where each team member's strengths lie, as well as figure out ways to organize their time and their roles so they can play to their strengths most of the time. Good teams are well rounded, precisely because each individual team member is not.

Of course, this doesn't mean that we don't have to address an area of weakness to ensure we're not putting our team at risk, or even just step outside our own zone of greatness and "take one" for the team sometimes. Every team has these needs from time to time. A good team member will help others understand their strengths and deliberately volunteer these strengths (rather than their weaknesses) to the rest of the team so they can regularly access a state of flow and perform at their very best.

The good news is, studies suggest that seventy-three percent of us use at least one of our strengths once a week.[8] So, even if your moments of flow at work feel brief and rare, finding ways to build on these strengths will help you leverage those things you're already motivated to do; that you have the neural wiring to support; and that your workplace is encouraging, enabling and rewarding in some way.

Remember, building on your strengths is all about finding what's already working, and looking for ways you can do more of it. The easy way to figure this out is by completing a stream-of-consciousness audit of your moments of flow at work by completing the play sheet provided. Trust us—it'll take far less time than rewriting your resume and looking for a new job. In Michelle's experience of coaching hundreds of people in developing their strengths, when we dig below the initial dissatisfaction, exhaustion, and frustration that sometimes comes with our jobs, there are often more moments of flow occurring than you might expect. You have the opportunity to create more of these than you might imagine.

Case In Point

By Michelle McQuaid

When Melinda first came to me for coaching, she was a middle-level marketing manager at a pharmaceutical company who was struggling with her job. She was delivering what was expected and slowly working her way up the corporate ladder, but as the days passed, she found her work was becoming less and less enjoyable.

While she had the results to request a promotion to upper management, she just wasn't sure this was the work she wanted to be doing anymore. As a result, her career was going around in circles, and she was becoming increasingly dissatisfied, frustrated, and fed up about her work.

Initially, Melinda had decided that the only answer was to quit her job and find something that better suited her strengths. Before deciding if that was the best course of action, I suggested that perhaps it was worth digging a little deeper into what was really happening in her current work so that at least she didn't wind up in a similar situation.

When Melinda completed the VIA Survey, we discovered that her top five character strengths were *honesty, love, creativity, kindness,* and *curiosity.* As we reflected on her best moments at work—those times when she was really in flow and striking the golden mean of her strengths—it was clear that her strengths of honesty, love, and creativity were needed to nurture and develop teams in order to create marketing campaigns that would help people find better ways to care for their health and deliver business results. Would it be possible to create more of these moments in Melinda's day?

The challenge was that the management responsibilities of her role also required her to endure tedious rounds of meetings, complete an endless list of human resources paperwork, and comply with a growing burden of financial processes. These tasks had her reeling between boredom and anxiety, depending on the expected complexity, the impending deadline, and how fiercely her boss was driving her for completion. They left her feeling drained and disheartened, and were taking up more and more of her time. Would it be possible to make these moments less taxing, more engaging, and more effective so Melinda would be free to spend more time doing what she really enjoyed?

Melinda decided to try to approach these management tasks by being more mindful of her strengths.

She realized she was possibly underplaying her strengths of *kindness* and *curiosity* in meetings. To address this, she decided to take more interest in what her colleagues were saying in meetings and reflect on how her team's efforts may be able to better support other areas of the business. It didn't make every meeting enjoyable, but by becoming more interested in the content and making the effort to ask questions to better understand the implications for her team, it did make the time fly by more quickly. Melinda also had some helpful, "aha" moments about what her team could be doing to improve results.

Melinda also realized that she was possibly overplaying her strength of *love* by trying to capture every nuance of each of her staff members when completing some of the human-resources paperwork, making this more tedious than necessary. She gave her staff regular feedback as they were going about their jobs, so while their annual performance reports should be a fair reflection of these thoughts, it probably didn't require hours and hours of work. The human-resources paperwork was far less demanding when she added a time limit to appropriately apply her strength of love to the requirements of the tasks. Upon receiving their first "new-and-improved" performance reports, several of Melinda's team members noted how much easier it was to absorb and act on her more-focused and succinct feedback.

Finally, Melinda decided to reframe the dreaded financial processes, which she saw as a waste of time and an imposition on her creativity. By engaging her strength of *honesty* in a new way, Melinda instead viewed the financial processes as something that would ensure that her team had the resources they needed to continue creating great campaigns. Don't get me wrong—by reframing the financial processes in this way, Melinda didn't suddenly open these spreadsheets with a cry of "whoop-pee!" But she did find it easier to complete what needed to be done quickly and effectively by focusing on how it created freedom for her team, rather than telling herself over and over how much she hated wasting time on filling in these stupid numbers.

As the weeks went by, Melinda started to find that the burden of these dreaded tasks lightened a little. And, as she experienced more moments of flow at work, her energy and enthusiasm started to return. Not all at once, and not all the time—change is rarely instantaneous or ubiquitous. But, as Melinda became more confident about her choices regarding how she completed what was expected of her, she started to see new possibilities to find the flow experiences she longed for. Six months later, she was promoted and was exceeding all expectations—even her own— after teaching her team how to also develop their strengths.

Flow Audit Play Sheet

Use this play sheet to get a sense of what's really happening in your work and of what's really possible when it comes to using your strengths in a state of flow. While you've already discovered your strengths and what they look like in their golden mean, we want to broaden your scope of inquiry to all of your work—not just specific moments—and anchor it in your *current* job.

Try to complete this exercise as if you're brainstorming. Don't over-think your answers. Rather, let it be a stream of consciousness—with no wrong answers—and see what surfaces. You might even want to set a time limit of twenty minutes on this activity.

1. List your top five character strengths (or talents if using Gallup StrengthsFinder; or unrealized strengths if using Realise2) on the chart. Then start with your first strength and brainstorm::

    •   How and where do you use this strength in a state of flow—those times when you feel like you're in the zone or one with the music—in your current role? Be sure to draw on your discovery answers to help anchor those generic descriptions into your real world.

    •   How often do you feel like you get to use this strength in a state of flow—neither underplayed nor overplayed—at work?

    •   What are the ways you could create more moments of flow in your job by finding the golden mean of this strength more frequently?

    •   What changes might you need to make to ensure that you use this strength more frequently? Is it scheduling a regular time, getting development support to avoid underplaying or overplaying the strength, adjusting the focus of your role, or seeking permission?

    •   What outcomes might you achieve if these changes were made and you started using this strength more frequently?

Flow Audit Play Sheet (continued)

2. Complete Step 1 for each of your remaining top five strengths. Remember, this is a stream of consciousness, so don't stop to edit it, judge it, or re-phrase it. Just give voice to your top-of-mind thoughts and feelings, and then we'll discuss this in the next part of this chapter

Strength	When do you use it in flow?	How often do you use it in flow?	How could you use it more?	What changes do you need?	What outcomes might result?
1.		____ Daily ____ Every few days ____ Weekly ____ Monthly ____ Very rarely; ____ Never			
2.		____ Daily ____ Every few days ____ Weekly ____ Monthly ____ Very rarely; ____ Never			
3.		____ Daily ____ Every few days ____ Weekly ____ Monthly ____ Very rarely; ____ Never			
4.		____ Daily ____ Every few days ____ Weekly ____ Monthly ____ Very rarely; ____ Never			
5.		____ Daily ____ Every few days ____ Weekly ____ Monthly ____ Very rarely; ____ Never			

Connecting Strengths to Your Purpose

When it comes to designing a strengths-fueled future, it's relatively simple to think of ways to apply your strengths in the pursuit of work that is bigger, faster, and stronger. But before you do that, we want to give you the space to just pause for a few moments and really think about what your strength-fueled future is for.

You see, studies have found that when we set life goals around money, power, and popularity—what researchers call "profit goals"—even when we achieve these goals, they generally leave us feeling no more satisfied or confident about ourselves. What does seem to change are the number of negative indicators in wellbeing like stress, anxiety, and even depression.[9] This is because often we're pursuing these goals to meet someone else's expectations of us; they're "have to" goals driven by our extrinsic motivations for reward and recognition.

But when we set life goals around growth, connection, and contribution— what the researchers call "purpose goals"—not only do they leave us feeling more satisfied and confident upon their accomplishment, they also improve our wellbeing. We pursue these goals because they're connected to our sense of purpose; they're "want to" goals driven by intrinsic motivations for meaning and pleasure.[10]

Now don't get us wrong—we're not saying there is anything wrong with money, power, or popularity, provided you're pursuing them for the right reasons. After all, a nun who's in her job for the wrong reasons is likely to have lower wellbeing than an investment banker who's in her job for the right reasons.

Before you rush off to create a strengths-fueled future, it pays to understand what you want and why. This understanding will make it easier to maintain your motivation for the journey, and it'll help move you toward the career and life you really want to be living. As John F. Kennedy once said, "Effort and courage are not enough without purpose and direction."

So what inspires your work beyond your need to just make money? What gives you a sense of fulfillment or purpose? What will cause you to leap out of bed in the morning? What compass will guide the ways you want to develop your strengths so you can create the career you're craving?

Finding Something Bigger Than Yourself

Your purpose doesn't have to be world-changing, although there is nothing wrong with that. Your purpose just has to give you a sense of meaning. There are 101 different ways you can make money, so why have you chosen this particular option? And if by chance you're sitting there as Michelle was several years ago thinking that a purpose sounds nice but is not really something you can afford right now, let us share one of her favorite stories:

> A man passes three men breaking up stones by the side of the road. He asks the first man, "What are you doing?"
>
> The first man replies, "Breaking stones into rocks."
>
> He asks the second man, "What are you doing?"
>
> The second man replies, "Feeding my family."
>
> And finally he asks the third man, "What are you doing?"
>
> The third man replies, "Building a cathedral."

Often when we link a sense of purpose to our work, we assume that we have to be engaged in some great and noble endeavor. But it's important not to ignore the small daily differences you can make which, over time, add up to big ones. No matter what your job, you can draw meaning from it. Consider the following example from a study by Yale psychologist Amy Wrzesniewski. Hospital janitors—whose responsibilities were to sweep the floors, dust, and empty the wastebaskets—either described their work as a job that paid their bills, or as a career that would lead them to other opportunities. However, almost one-third instead saw their tasks as a "calling" which helped people to recover from illnesses by ridding the hospital of dangerous germs. This not only made their job more bearable, but also more engaging and enjoyable.[11]

Leadership researcher and author Simon Sinek notes that most of us are pretty clear on "what" we do each day, and even "how" we go about it—but few of us can articulate "why" we do the things we do.[12] The challenge is that your motivation and willingness to act—in this case, to start developing your strengths—comes from your "why," not from your "what" or your "how."

There are many different pathways you can explore to find your "why." Based on Michelle's experience, we find the *Best Possible Self Exercise*, created by Professor Laura King, to be one of the most effective tools for working on strengths-development. This exercise helps to boost your level of optimism, clarify your goals, and improve your confidence to follow through on them. Clients write expressively about themselves to weave together their strength discoveries and their flow audit. This enables them to design a clear and compelling vision of what might be possible when it comes to developing their strengths at work in ways that are meaningful and fulfilling to them. [13]

Now, some of you might be ready to tackle the play sheet at the end of this chapter. Others might be inwardly groaning and wondering if now would be a good time to flip ahead to the next chapter. Either way, we want you to take a moment and pause, because what we're about to share with you ensures that the changes you're trying to make will finally start sticking.

Are you ready?

Being Pulled by the Future

Positive images pull us forward into positive actions. As Professor David Cooperrider—one of the world's leading researchers in creating positive change—taught us, positive images pull us forward into new possibilities that fuel us with hope and put us on the road to finding solutions, helping us to realize we have the power to make things happen.[14]

How does this work? Just the very idea of having the rewards that come from getting something that we're hoping for is enough to kick-start a cascade of dopamine—our brain's reward drug—through key neural pathways in the brain that have the power to move us from intention to action.[15]

For example, for decades, the four-minute mile was considered a natural limit for runners. It was unthinkable to go faster. Then English athlete Roger Bannister set himself the impossible goal, started training accordingly, and in May 1954, he shattered this barrier on an Oxford track. Within three years, sixteen other runners had also surpassed this "human" limit. There was no fundamental leap in human evolution. What had changed was their ability to imagine what was possible.[16]

Studies on the placebo phenomenon in medicine suggest anywhere from one-third to two-thirds of medical drug-trial patients show marked physiological and emotional improvements in symptoms simply by believing they were being given an effective treatment—even when that treatment was just a sugar pill or some other inert substance. While the complex mind-body pathways that create this result are far from being resolved, there is one area of clear agreement medically: positive changes in anticipatory reality, through suggestion and belief, play a central role in all placebo responses.[17]

Positive images pull us forward into positive action. Perhaps this is why Albert Einstein once famously said, "Imagination is more important than knowledge." And, it may be why Seligman has more recently focused his research on the science of "prospection" and our ability to make mental simulations about the future that draw us forward. Proposing that intelligence is not what you know, but how well you simulate the future and act on your predictions, Seligman believes this is what gives humans the edge over other species. Rather than thinking of people as prisoners of the past, he envisions a new field of study that focuses on imagination and getting better at moving into the future.[18]

Now, if you're feeling a little nervous about moving into the future and committing your most heartfelt hopes to paper, don't despair. It's natural to feel a little scared about giving voice to our deepest-held desires, because it makes it harder to deny the changes we want to be making. In fact, fear is the number-one emotion that stops us from living the lives we most want.[19] Fear that we're not good enough. Fear that we're not worthy. Fear of what might happen if we succeed. Fear that it might all fall apart.

Fear keeps us small, and stuck in jobs that don't fulfill us but that feel safe. But is there really anything safe about living a life where you feel disengaged, disillusioned, or desperate to be doing something other than what you're doing? Do you really want to live in the shadows of your own life?

Here's the thing—there is a big difference between being well-off and having wellbeing. It's easy to mislead ourselves into thinking that if we just had the success we wanted, then it would be simple to develop our strengths to show up and shine in ways that truly matter. But it actually works in reverse. We believe that only when you know what truly matters to you will you develop your strengths to show up in the ways that matter, shine in the things that count, and succeed in the areas you most value.

And it starts by getting honest about the life you really want to be living, no matter what it might require you to start risking. After all, every worthwhile endeavor requires us to risk something. Try heeding the word of Marianne Williamson: "Our deepest fear is not that we are inadequate. Our deepest fear is that we're powerful beyond measure. It is our light, not our darkness, that most frightens us. We ask ourselves who am I to be brilliant, gorgeous, talented, and fabulous. Actually, who are you not to be?"

Complete the play sheet below to discover your strengths-fueled best-possible future self, and read the next chapter to discover the tested way you can turn these hopes into your new reality.

Case In Point

By Michelle McQuaid

When I first started imagining a strengths-fueled future in my work, I was in a role where my sense of purpose—other than feeding my family—was pretty thin on the ground. Our goal was to make money for the people who owned the business by serving our clients well. And, after having helped line their pockets for several years, I was finding it harder and harder to get out of bed just to make them even richer.

To try to improve my levels of engagement, I'd been developing my strengths and trying to find more moments of flow by hitting my golden mean for a little while. Work had definitely improved, but I still wasn't leaping out of bed. I needed a purpose that was going to give me a greater sense of meaning and fulfillment so I could stay in the job and continue to financially support my family.

As I reviewed my flow audit and the rare moments of engagement I was experiencing, I used an idea from Dr. Tal Ben Shahar, Harvard's first positive psychology lecturer, and started looking to explicitly define the meaning I found in these activities. I did this by asking: What's the purpose of this task? What does that accomplish? If the answer still didn't feel meaningful, I'd ask again: What does that accomplish? And if this answer still seemed unfulfilling I'd ask again: What does that accomplish? Until eventually I'd reach an "aha!"

For example, I experienced moments of flow when using my strength of hope to coach my team members and improve their performance. It wasn't the technical skills of copy writing or online marketing that I was teaching them that gave these moments meaning. Rather, it was finding ways to help bring out the best in others that made this so enjoyable for me. What if I started to focus more of my energy at work into using everything I was learning about human flourishing to nurture and develop my team? What if, in the process, the tasks that needed completing were achieved?

Now that was an idea I'd be willing to leap out of bed for! As I completed the Best Possible Self exercise, I saw a strengths-fueled future where I could more easily, effectively, and joyfully meet and exceed the expectations of my job. I'd do this by using my strengths of curiosity, creativity, and hope to find ways to bring out the best in myself and my team no matter what tasks we were doing.

The more I started to show up each day and use this "why" as the compass to guide "how" and "what" I did, the more fulfilling I started to find my previously soulless occupation. Even though I was a little nervous at first about whether the work that had to be delivered would still get done, what surprised me the most was that when I stopped fixating on "what" I did each day, both my team and I started performing better.

Now, don't get me wrong, I wasn't saving the world or doing anything spectacular. But as my team shared how they were using some of the ideas I was teaching them with their family and friends (like spotting their strengths) and describing the difference this was making in their lives, I finally felt like my work and life were moving in the direction I wanted to be taking.

Best Possible Future Self Play Sheet

What would your strengths-fueled, best-possible future self look like?

1. Select a point in your future career that is far enough ahead in time that you have space to create some lasting changes, but is not so far away that it feels like what you do now doesn't matter. It might be six months, a year, three years from now . . . whatever feels right for you.

2. Then (after reading this), close your eyes, take a few deep, slow breaths, and just imagine that everything—everything—has gone as well as it possibly could and that you're using the golden mean of your strengths consistently at work to create more and more of those moments you identified in your flow audit. And as you imagine this, think about

    •   Why are you leaping out of bed to get to work each morning? What is the growth, connection and/or contribution you're making that allows you to achieve the "want-to" goals you're craving? How does it feel to have chosen to spend your time and energy on this work? Why are you proud to tell others about the impact of your work?

    •   How are you using your strengths each day to make your "why" a reality? How does it feel to be hitting the golden mean of your strengths regularly? What do your colleagues say about working with you now?

    •   What are you prioritizing to do each day at work? What are the tasks you really look forward to undertaking? Who is working on them with you? What do your clients or bosses say about the quality of your work?

Try to imagine this future as realistically and vividly as possible. What are you thinking, seeing, hearing, doing, and feeling in this new world? What are the things that others notice, comment on,

Best Possible Future Self Play Sheet (continued)

and value in you? The more descriptive and specific you can make it, the stronger this exercise will be in pulling you forward.

3. After you have a fairly clear image in your mind of how things might unfold, spend about twenty minutes writing down the details in a stream of consciousness. Don't edit them. Don't second-guess them. Don't judge them. Just let them flow out.

4. If you can, repeat this process for the following two days as well. It's a great way to really dig into your most hidden needs and kick your creativity into gear about ways you can create a purpose-driven, strengths-fueled future at work.

CHAPTER 5

How Can You Design Pathways to Move Forward?

When you have a vision for the future and your best possible future self, you can't help but be pulled forward by life. When you're excited about "what's next," it helps you to see beyond your current challenges, it frees up your energy to invest more in moving forward, and you start to see opportunities opening up that will help you to realize these new possibilities. Your new narrative about the future starts to compete with the old stories that have held your career back.

You can improve your levels of motivation to move forward by tapping into your freedom to choose your own pathways, leveraging your strengths to bolster your sense of competence, and seeking support from others. When these basic psychological needs are met, research suggests it enhances your creativity, performance, and wellbeing, making your dreams more accessible.[1]

In this chapter, we'll show you the three simple steps you can take to turn your hopes into reality by setting clear goals—identifying multiple strategies to move you from where you are to where you want to be, overcoming obstacles, and maintaining your willpower for the journey. We promise that this is a tested, simple, and painless approach that has worked for thousands of people. Just trust the process.

Hoping For a Strengths-Fueled Future

While eighty-nine percent of us believe tomorrow will be better than today, only fifty percent of us believe we can make it so.[2] Scientists believe this is the difference between wishing and hoping. When we simply wish that tomorrow will be better than today, we take a passive role. That is, we believe the details of how this will unfold are beyond our control. But when we hope that tomorrow will be better than today and believe we can make it so, we feel compelled to act on our high expectations of the future while being realistic about the obstacles we may encounter.

Hopeful people understand that the way from the present to the future is rarely a straight line, and almost never one single line. They believe there are many paths to their goals and understand it's unlikely any of them are free of obstacles. Consequently, they play and experiment with multiple strategies, and they plan for difficulties, setbacks, and disappointments to ensure they're resilient enough to reach their goals.[3]

Cultivating Hope

Hope occurs when your rational self meets your emotional self in a three-part process that helps to carry you to a better future:

- **"Want-to" goals:** Hope starts by identifying where you want to go, what you want to accomplish, and who you want to be. In other words, hope is built from the goals that matter most to you because these fill your mind with pictures of the future.

- **Multiple pathways:** Hope involves the formulation of multiple pathways to reach your goals. These are the plans that carry you forward, help you navigate the obstacles, and enable you to monitor your progress. They're often described as "way power" because they help you find your way forward.

- **"Agency":** Hope entails a drive to make things happen. This is your perceived ability to your shape your life. It's your willingness to take responsibility for moving toward your goals. It's often described as "willpower," as it builds your capacity for persistence and long-term effort.[4]

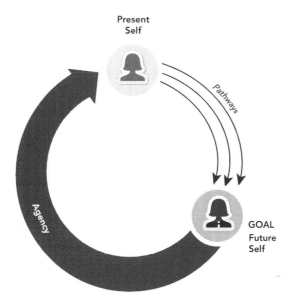

Each of these parts works as a continuous feedback loop, setting the next part in motion and forming a cycle that enhances hope. In the sweet spot of this cycle, you listen to your desires and dreams because they tell you who you are, and you notice the strengths you have that others might miss. You believe in your ability to make the future better than the present, while at the same time you recognize the limits of your control. You devote time and effort to the strengths you need to develop, and understand the difference between negativity—which creates doubt and saps your energy—and helpful critiques.

Shane Lopez, the world's leading researcher on hope, describes it like this: "Hope is created moment by moment through our deliberate choices. It happens when we use our thoughts and feelings to temper our aversion to loss and actively pursue what is possible. When we choose hope, we define what matters to us most."[5]

Studies that have investigated hope suggest that how we think about the future is a key determinant of success in school, work, and life. Other conditions being equal, it has been shown that hope can lead to a fourteen-percent bump in workplace outcomes and a ten-percent boost in happiness. It enables us to show-up, be more productive, boost our wellbeing, cultivate more meaning in our lives, and enjoy better health. Hope has also been found to help us focus on our long-term goals so we can make better short-term choices and regulate our behaviors. Best of all, when it comes to making our dreams a reality, hope gives us the energy to make things happen.[6]

Challenging Your Beliefs

How does hope achieve all of this? It turns out that hope is neither a psychological silver spoon nor a by-product of our IQ. Rather, Lopez and his colleagues have concluded that hope comes from our energy and excitement about what's next. This is why Stanford psychologist, Professor Carol Dweck, has found that more important than believing in your abilities is the belief that you can *improve* your abilities.

Dweck's research suggests there are two possible ways—two "mindsets"—to think about the future, which will predict our likelihood of success. To see which mindset you hold and how this might impact your levels of hope, make a note if you've experienced any of these feelings about your work:

- Anxiety at taking on new challenges or roles for fear that people will discover you're not as good as they thought.

- Pain—emotionally or physically—when hearing negative feedback about yourself because you're really not sure you can do any better.

- Dread that mistakes you've made will be discovered, because you worry that failure may be fatal to your career.

- Desire to control as much around you as you possibly can to ensure that your work is successfully delivered.

- An obsessive drive to achieve the desired outcomes and prove you can be successful.

These feelings suggest an underlying belief that things like your talent and intelligence are largely fixed and there's not much you can really do to improve upon them. At heart, you believe people are born "clever" or "dumb," "sporty" or "un-coordinated," "gifted" or "ordinary," "winners" or "losers"—although you may never say this to anyone. As a result, you have a tendency, even if it's subconscious, to measure people by the outcomes they achieve, rather than the efforts they put in. Dweck calls this a *"fixed mindset."*

Now, don't take this to mean that you can't, or haven't, achieved great things. Highly driven Type-A personalities who like to be perceived as "experts" often exhibit this mindset. The problem Dweck has found is that the constant stress and anxiety of both success and failure causes people with a fixed mindset to eventually plateau and fall short of reaching their true potential.[7]

Why? Well, if you have a fixed mindset, you are less hopeful about the future. You have an upper limit, and there's nothing you can do to change it, so why try? You're more likely to miss cues about where you need to make more effort or develop your strengths to move ahead. And when you strike obstacles, you're more likely to give up—feeling helpless and hopeless that you simply don't have the resources required.

But perhaps you've also experienced other feelings about your work. Again, make a note of any of the following feelings that ring true to you—and don't feel dismayed if you've noted things from both the previous list and the following list:

- Hope and excitement at taking on new challenges at work because of the opportunity for growth and development.

- Curiosity when listening to critical feedback about yourself with a desire to discover what you can do to improve and get better.

- Willingness to take responsibility for your failures because you accept that getting things wrong is a natural part of the learning process.

- Courage to keep showing up and trying because this is the real measure of success.

These feelings suggest an underlying belief that things like your talent and intelligence can be built up with practice to a point of mastery. This is something that neuroscience now lends strong support to. As a result, you have a tendency, even if it's subconscious, to focus more on effort and learning as the true measure of a person. Think about Thomas Edison and his infamous quote about finally inventing the light bulb: "I didn't fail, I just found 10,000 ways it didn't work." Dweck calls this a *"growth mindset."*

Dweck's research suggests that this mindset influences our ability to set goals, to seek help, and to be motivated to achieve what matters most to us.

Ultimately, she has found that our mindset determines our levels of self-belief, the outcomes we achieve, and our wellbeing. A growth mindset sparks hope by helping us to feel like we have nothing to lose—and much to gain—if we try new ways to reach our goals. Your inner voice says something like, "No matter what I start with, I can develop or find the resources I need as challenges pop up." A growth mindset helps you move beyond your present limitations and as a result, you're able to achieve ever-higher levels of success.[8]

If you found yourself noting down feelings you've had at work from both the fixed and growth mindset lists, don't despair. For most of us, these mindsets are not black and white. For example, you might find that you have a largely fixed mindset when it comes to dealing with your boss, but you may have a growth mindset when dealing with your peers. When it comes to management responsibilities, you might have quite a fixed mindset and be fearful of making mistakes, but in the area of technical knowledge, you have a growth mindset and are always keen to learn and explore new ideas. The good news is that no matter how much your fixed mindset might currently dominate your work, there are several very simple steps you can take to leverage a growth mindset instead. It starts with the "want-to" goals you set.

Case In Point

By Michelle McQuaid

It's time to confess—I spent most of my career in a fixed mindset. When presented with new challenges and opportunities at work, I could constantly hear that little voice chattering away inside my head with stories like, "You're not good enough to pull this off," "Everyone will find out it's just been good luck up to now," or, "You'll be exposed for the imposter you are."

Although my fear of failure was poisonously potent, my fear of not being somebody who mattered was even greater. It was very clear that I believed that outcomes were the true measure of a person. I judged people—including myself—by the job titles they had, the organizations they worked for, the money they earned, the opportunities they were given, and they accolades they won.

As a result of really wanting to do well at work, I felt it safest to keep a tight control on as many things as possible. Why delegate tasks to someone else when I could do it quicker and better myself? Why not work as many hours as humanly possible if it meant doing something really well? What was wrong with striving for perfection, no matter what the cost, if it delivered an exceptional outcome?

Most people who worked with me had no idea all this stress was bubbling away just under the surface. To the outside world, I appeared calm and confident. Like a duck gliding across a pond, it was all serenity and grace on the surface, but underneath I was paddling for my life. The only time people glimpsed what might really be going on was when I crumpled in the face of failure or negative feedback.

The shame of being found to be not good enough, and believing there was nothing I could really do to improve upon my abilities, was enough to bring me to my knees. The pain of not being able to do all I wanted, and the belief that this would negatively impact my dreams, left me feeling completely spent and helpless. Eventually, the fear of not being someone who mattered had me simply ignoring constructive feedback and instead just wishing that next time I would do better.

And, despite all of this, I didn't do too badly. But by the time I became the global brand director for one of the world's largest firms, the constant fear of both success and failure had left me drained, disheartened, and exhausted. I couldn't imagine going forward, nor could I bear to go back. Surely, there had to be a better way to live.

When I discovered Dweck's research on fixed mindsets, it was like looking into a mirror. I remember thinking to myself, *Oh there you are. I had no idea all of this was going on inside me.* No wonder I'm a mess. The relief at realizing it wasn't just me who heard these voices, and that I didn't have to accept these fear-based stories, opened up a whole new world of possibilities in how I went about my work.

I started tuning in to the stories I was telling myself and how they made me feel and act. When they didn't serve me well, I began to ask, "Is that true? Is that the only explanation?" As I practiced generating alternative scenarios, I noticed each one made me a little different and opened up new paths for action. Having decided to value effort and learning over outcomes, it became easier and easier to take the growth mindset option.

As I built this skill up, it became quicker and easier to catch my stories, reframe them, and respond in ways I was proud of. My stress levels declined dramatically, and my energy returned as I started to get excited about what might be next. As my confidence grew, I knew that no matter what challenge or opportunity I was faced with, all I needed to do was show up, give it my best effort, and be willing to learn along the way. Not surprisingly, most of my anxiety about work melted away.

Don't get me wrong, I still wanted to deliver good things for my employer. But my own identity was no longer tied to these results, which allowed me to hold my responsibilities more lightly. It made me willing to delegate responsibilities to others because I accepted that this was how we'd all grow. It made me want to invest in my wellbeing so I had the energy to show up consistently and keep learning. It made me focus on the journey rather than just the destination, which helped me to be more open and flexible in the ways I went about my tasks.

It removed the pain and shame from failure and criticism. And while I doubt I'll ever run open-armed and excitedly toward my team to express my failures, I willingly shared my "screw up of the week" so my team would be able to see that mistakes are just part of learning.

In the years that followed, I went on to achieve success beyond my wildest dreams. I got promoted to the top of my field without ever having to ask for it. When I was ready to leave my organization, I was able to negotiate my own terms of exit, and for the past two years I've run my own business in what's arguably one of the toughest economies we've ever been in. I share this not to boast—my achievements are truly not what define me anymore—but to show you that while it may feel counterintuitive to prioritize being a "learner" over being an "expert," the psychological, intellectual, social, and physical freedoms that a growth mindset brings opens a whole new world of possibilities when it comes to your work.

Setting Growth Mindset Goals

No matter where you're starting, you can engage a growth mindset to shape your "want-to" goals and create the strengths-fueled future you've imagined. Start by tuning in to the feelings you have and stories you're telling yourself about your ability to make your dream a reality. Are these stories pulling you forward toward your dreamed possibilities, because you believe that as long as you put in your best effort, willingly practice your strengths, and stay open to learning, you can make this a reality? Or are these stories causing you to hesitate and hold yourself back for fear that you might not be good enough to realize what you've imagined. Or even worse, what if you succeed and then can never top it?

If the latter stories are haunting you, start by tuning in to these feelings and what you're telling yourself about your abilities. Then pause and ask yourself, "Is that true?"

What you might not realize is that your brain is a sense-making machine and it's happiest when all the pieces of the puzzle fit together. One of the ways you try to fulfill this need is by making sense of what might happen next by telling yourself stories. And although sometimes these stories are completely accurate, most of the time they're not.[9]

You see, when your fixed mindset sparks fear about your limitations, it's like you have blinders on and can only see the most obvious options that allow you to escape what scares you. In contrast, when you challenge these fears and allow your growth mindset to spark hope about your possibilities, this fires up your creativity to find pathways forward and broadens your thinking because it fuels your persistence.[10]

For example, is "I'm not good enough" the only explanation of what might happen if I take this project on? Or maybe there's a great team around me who will provide the support to reach the desired result? Even if I don't deliver every expected outcome, this still could be a great experience for me.

By challenging your stories, you gain the power to choose the "want-to" goals that:

- Help you feel willing to show up in ways that will serve you best in different situations for the outcomes you want.

- Free you in the here and now so you can enjoy the journey and not just the result.

- Are aligned to the purpose of growth, contribution, and connection so they don't restrict you or hang over your head, but liberate you to find the golden mean of your strengths at work regularly and realize your best possible future self.

When setting your "want-to" goals, it helps to be specific. Don't settle for "I want to be happier at work." What are you going to do that will make you happier? How will it support your growth, contribution, and connection to others? Why will what you deliver be valued?

You will also boost your energy if you can state your goals positively to add to your life rather than subtract from it. "I want to stop doing work I don't enjoy" is clear enough, but the negative focus will make it hard to find the energy to take action. "I want to connect a network of credible, inspiring, and collaborative people to explore new ways we can go to market" is an additive goal—it adds a positive behavior to make your work more enjoyable.[11]

Good goals are like looking through a pair of binoculars. They make fuzzy distant objects much clearer. To help select the first goal on your journey, try using the Cantril's Ladder (named after the psychologist who created it) exercise. Imagine a ladder with steps numbered from zero at the bottom to ten at the top. The top of the ladder represents the best possible future self you've imagined in the last chapter. The bottom of the ladder represents the worst possible life for you. On which step of the ladder would you say you stand at this time? Now on which step would you be excited to stand twelve months from now? What clear, specific, additive goal does this suggest you should set yourself?

Turning Hopes into Action

When it comes to moving from where you are today to where you want to be tomorrow, research recommends that it's worth having a plan A, B, and even C. That way, even if you encounter insurmountable obstacles on the path, it doesn't mean you have to forego the goal you're trying to reach. Studies suggest we're far more successful at following through on the pathways we've chosen if we plan for the obstacles up front.[12] In this way, they won't throw us into such disarray and undermine your efforts and willpower to reach your long-term goal.

The good news is that your brain is already constantly creating and revising these mental maps to help you navigate your way through the world. They start with an "I am Here" point (the status quo), from which a variety of paths radiate outward, the number depending on the complexity of the decision, and the clarity of your thinking at the moment. The most successful decisions come when we are thinking clearly and creatively enough to recognize all the paths available to us.[13]

One of the best ways to uncover these pathways is to give yourself permission to play with the possibilities so you can open your mind to new ideas, and experiment with new ways of being and new ways to develop your strengths at work.[14] That's right, we're urging you to *play* with your work.

Play is a natural form of problem solving that gives you the chance to make sense of the world—and your role in it—by letting you try out new identities, strategies, and possibilities for how to move ahead. Think of it is a life-size simulator that allows you to explore different "what-if" scenarios when it comes to developing your strengths and how you might handle them in the safest possible way. It allows you to move beyond the limitations that have kept you stuck, and propels you forward to discover pathways you never thought existed.[15]

If you're struggling to play, "sentence stem completion" is a technique many people find helpful. Thought to help us access the hidden wisdom of our subconscious mind, there are a few basic rules to guide you with this exercise. Try to write down quickly at least six endings—or as many as you can think of—to the sentence stem. Put aside your critical mind; think after, not during. There are no right or wrong answers, as long as they grammatically complete the sentence stem. It's fine if some of your answers contradict each other. Simply generate your responses, then go over them and see whether you have learned anything important; it may take a few trials before you gain the pathways you think worthy of exploration.[16]

Try completing these sentence stems as quickly and with as many endings as possible:

- Over the next six months, if I operated five percent more purposefully at work, I would . . .

- Over the next six months, if I used my strengths five percent more at work, I could . . .

- Over the next six months, I could get five percent closer to the goal I've set by . . .

- Over the next six months, I could make my work five percent more enjoyable if I . . .

- If any of what I've written is true, pathways I might prioritize include . . .

You'll find that pathways are plentiful when you're willing to take risks and fear doesn't dampen your creativity and courage.

No matter what approach you use to design your pathways forward, the aim is to shrink your goal into smaller, more manageable, concrete steps that help you develop your strengths and build your confidence. Try to be as specific as possible about the "where," "when," and "how" of these steps so you know exactly what you need to be doing to reach your goal.[17] For example, "I'll use my strength of curiosity over the next month to compile a list of credible, inspiring, and collaborative people and then invite them to join my network."

It also helps to be mindful about which aspects of your goal you have control over and which ones you don't. Some things will be in your control, and other things are going to take a bit of luck, good timing, and possibly some unexpected support along the way. Make sure that you're investing your efforts where they're going to have the most impact and try to let go of the rest.[18] Again, you'll find that a growth mindset really helps with this step.

Plan B'ing—or finding your way power—is made stronger with practice, so think about the goal you chose earlier. What are the small, manageable, concrete steps that will develop your strengths? Is it within your control and will it move you closer to your goal? That's Plan A. What's Plan B? And Plan C? Are these the best plans you can think of? Do they leverage your strengths?

Maintaining Your Willpower

By and large, we all want to pursue goals that are in our best interest, but even when we feel really committed to making positive changes, sustaining them for any length of time can be challenging. We get distracted, life interrupts us, we become too busy, and we run out of energy. Before we know it, the pathways we've chosen have slipped away. We wish that our willpower and self-control would help us keep moving forward, but when it comes to following through on our good intentions, most of us run out of steam.[19]

The truth is, making your hopes a reality will require committed and dedicated effort. Just like eating one piece of broccoli isn't suddenly going to make you healthy, or going for a run won't mean that you're fit, your pathways will require regular weekly—or even daily—efforts to create the strengths-fueled future you've imagined.[20] Drawing on your strengths will make pursuing the pathways easier, more engaging, and more effective—but achieving any goal also requires honest and regular monitoring of your progress. This allows you to savor and celebrate the changes you're creating, generating more positive emotions that keep pulling you forward. It also helps you see when a pathway may need tweaking to improve your results, or even when one pathway needs to be relinquished in favor of other pathways that are delivering better outcomes.[21] To help you, there are a growing range of online and smartphone apps that can monitor and measure your progress, such as *GoalsOnTrack*, *Lift*, and *Strides*.

Sticking to your pathways will also be much easier with the support of others. For example, studies have found that people who make New Year's resolutions are much more likely to persevere for at least two years if they have social support.[22] Your colleagues, boss, friends, and family can help motivate you, offer positive feedback, and appreciate the efforts you're making. If you can, lift your social support to a whole new level by associating with people who share your goals. This will give you an automatic boost in focus, a ready sounding board when you get stuck, and a means to galvanize your commitment and perseverance. It can also make the whole endeavor a lot more fun.

Finally, try to short-circuit the temptations that might throw you off your pathways. Research suggests this can be achieved by making a public commitment because you want to appear consistent with yourself and more accountable to yourself.[23] Lopez suggests going online to create a contract for change with yourself at stickK.com to make your goals public and binding. Created by Yale economists, on this website you'll select your goal, set your stakes (you place a bet, risking either your money or your good name), pick a referee (who monitors your commitment and progress), and build a support team to cheer you on.[24]

Being the author of your own life means knowing you can make things happen—or stop them from happening—to reach the "want-to" goals you've chosen. Hope is like oxygen; you can't live without it. As Martin Luther King once observed, "Everything that is done in the world, is done by hope." So what can you do to monitor your progress? Who can support you on this journey? How will you celebrate forward movement on your pathways? Will these continue to ignite the motivation and persistence you need to reach your goal?

Case In Point

By Michelle McQuaid

When I met Robert in a developing-strengths workshop, he had been working for a large bank for almost a decade and was struggling to find the energy to juggle a demanding job, a young family, and his own health. Based on his boss's feedback, Robert was invested in some very fixed mindset stories and the belief he needed to be working on his weaknesses so he could better think on his feet, put a point of view forward, and deliver more quickly. The daily pressure to make these changes left him feeling constantly worried about how others were judging his mistakes.

When Robert completed the VIA Survey, he discovered his signature strengths were *teamwork, judgment, kindness, fairness,* and *leadership*. He was a little surprised that the strength of *humor* and *playfulness* was not higher, as this had always been an essential part of his life. But on reflection, Robert realized that *humor* and *playfulness* was not valued in his current work environment. He was also disappointed that his strength of *social intelligence* was sitting just outside his top five strengths, but acknowledged that his boss's feedback had made him more inwardly focused rather than attuning to others.

After exploring how Robert was using his signature strengths and starting to understand what the golden mean and flow moments looked like in his work, it became clear that he really enjoyed coaching and developing others. He'd felt most alive when completing the first stage of an Executive Coaching Course the year before, so when he sat down to imagine his strengths-fueled best-possible self, he dreamed of having the *social intelligence, judgment,* and *kindness* to be a full-time executive coach who helped others in the bank. Robert also wanted to go home with his strengths of *zest* and *humor* intact so he could support and enjoy his young family.

With his future coming into focus, we decided to see if we could map his hopes onto a page to create a plan to move him from where he was to where he wanted to be.

Robert decided that the first "want-to" goal on his ladder would be to become certified and recognized as an executive coach who unleashed people's peak performances at the bank, while maintaining his own health and happiness within the next twelve months. It was clear. It was specific. It was purpose-focused.

Next, Robert identified three pathways to move toward this goal. First, he had to use his strength of *judgment* to find the right coaching program; his business case needed to be accepted; and he needed to complete the learning requirements to become a certified executive coach. Secondly, Robert had to use his strengths of *kindness* and *social intelligence* to more actively take up informal coaching opportunities within his team. Thirdly, to cultivate his strengths of *zest* and *humor*, Robert had to ensure that he was getting enough sleep, exercising regularly, and finding reasons to laugh. These were small, manageable, concrete steps that could draw on his strengths (some of them his signature strengths, and some lesser strengths he wanted to prioritize) and were almost entirely within his control.

To help him navigate possible obstacles, Robert captured what might get in the way of seeing each of these pathways through. For the first pathway, there was always the chance his boss might not approve or be able to fund the course. For the second pathway, there was the risk of remaining so focused on himself that Robert would miss the chance to coach others. For the third pathway, there was the challenge of making time to follow through on these new habits.

Finally, Robert wrote down ideas to maintain his willpower. He created an Excel chart to measure his progress. He asked an existing coach at the bank to be his mentor. He hired a fitness trainer to keep him accountable on his health. He recorded a score each day in his diary to monitor his energy levels and laughter. And each Friday, he made a thirty-minute coffee date with himself to reflect, celebrate, and savor on the choices he was making toward his goal. These small acts of accountability ensured that Robert could monitor his progress, rely on others for support, and recognize his own efforts.

It took Robert just seven months to complete his qualifications and be promoted to a coaching role at the bank. When it came to coaching others, he had no problems thinking on his feet, putting forward a point of view, or delivering quick results. When he started developing his strengths to do the coaching that allowed him to show up and shine in his work, it created an upward spiral of success in his work and in his life. Of all the hopes he realized, the one Robert cherished most was his new habit of spending the first fifteen minutes when he got home just playing and laughing with the children he loves.

Mapping Your Hopes Play Sheet

Lopez recommends mapping your hopes to help make your strengths-fueled future a reality. This play sheet will guide you through this activity and help put together all the things you've just learned.

Be sure to engage your growth mindset—challenge any of the stories that are holding you back and focus on the learning and development these hopes can unlock. Keep your strengths-discovery play sheet close at hand to find pathways that will be naturally engaging, energizing, and effective for you.

1. Imagine a ladder with steps numbered from zero at the bottom to ten at the top. The top of the ladder represents the best possible future self. The bottom of the ladder represents the worst possible life for you. On which step of the ladder would you say you are currently standing? Which step of the ladder would you be excited to stand on twelve months from now? What clear, specific, purpose-focused goal does this suggest you should set yourself? Write this down under the heading "Goal."

2. Think about the small, manageable, concrete steps you can take that will develop your strengths, are within your control, and will move you closer to your goal. If you're stuck, look back at your discovery play sheet for possible ideas, or try the sentence-stem completion technique on page 114. Remember, you want to find at least a Plan A, Plan B, and Plan C. Make sure each plan draws on the golden mean of one or more of your signature strengths or strengths you want to be developing.

3. For each pathway, note down the obstacles you might encounter that will keep you from achieving your goal. These might be related to time, resources, supporters, or other elements—either within or outside of your control. Be as honest as possible. Remember, studies suggest we're more likely to achieve our goals when we plan for the challenges we'll face upfront.

Mapping Your Hopes Play Sheet (continued)

4.   Around the edges of the page, record what you can do to maintain your willpower for this journey. How will you monitor your progress? Who will you ask for support? When and how will you celebrate your efforts to help you persevere?

5.   Put your map in a place where you can see it each day. This will help to give you the energy and confidence you need to create an upward spiral of success that propels you toward your strengths-fueled future.

Pathways	Obstacles	Goal
1.		
2.		
3.		

CHAPTER 6

How Can You Deliver Consistently on Your Strengths?

Now that you've discovered what your strengths look like, imagined your strengths-fueled future, and ignited the hope to move you from where you are to where you want to be, all that remains is to show up and do the work. But how will you fit this in with everything else that's going on in your day at the office? How will you find the time to prioritize developing your strengths on a daily basis even if it's not officially part of your job?

The good news is that when it comes to changing your behavior, studies suggest that small, regular actions are the best way to create lasting differences. This is because when you shrink the changes you want to create into tiny, busy-proof steps, you stop feeling overwhelmed and exhausted, and instead start notching-up success after success. As your confidence grows and your fear of failure withers, your progress begins to accumulate into a positive spiral of behavior.[1]

So if you're feeling a little overwhelmed right now, don't despair. In this chapter, we'll show you how you can develop your strengths in just eleven minutes each day, re-craft your job to help you spend more time doing what you do best, and build your levels of grit to ensure long-term success. We promise that you can make developing your strengths a daily gift that gives you the confidence and joy to show up, shine, and succeed just as you have dreamed.

Creating Time for Strengths

Researchers at Duke University estimate that up to forty percent of your actions each day are not conscious choices but mere habits—that's a little more than six hours![2] No wonder William James, the father of modern psychology, cautioned us almost a century ago that, "All our life, so far as it has definite form, is but a mass of habits—practical, emotional, and intellectual— systematically organized for our weal or our woe, and bearing us irresistibly towards our destiny, whatever the latter may be."

But let's be realistic—eighty percent of New Year's resolutions get broken every year because building positive habits can be hard work. Why? Because we think that when it comes to building ingrained life habits, we can go from zero to one hundred in an instant on the sheer force of willpower. Social psychologists have discovered that the problem with this approach is that the more we use our willpower over the course of a day, the more it wears out, making new habits difficult to sustain. In other words, our willpower is like a muscle that wears out.[3]

Luckily, researchers at MIT have found that there's a simple neurological loop at the core of every habit. The loop consists of three paths: a cue, a routine, and a reward.[4] Over time, this loop—cue, routine, reward, cue, routine, reward—becomes more and more automatic until a habit is born. By using this model to break a habit into these three components, it becomes possible to fiddle with the gears to make your strengths habits easier, more enjoyable, and lasting. It makes it possible to realize James's sage advice to "Make your nervous system your ally."

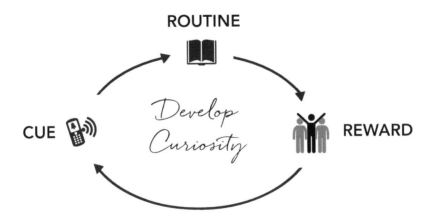

Creating a Cue

Studies have found that a cue can be almost anything, from a visual trigger such as a chocolate or a TV commercial, to a certain place, a time of day, an emotion, a sequence of thoughts, or the company of particular people. It just needs to be clear and simple.[5]

You can create a cue for a new habit by *anchoring* it to habits you already have. This way your existing habits—like getting out of bed each morning; traveling to work; turning on your computer; having your lunch; or getting ready to leave the office each night—act as a cue for your new habit.

You can also create a cue by *embedding* an action trigger in your environment so that you almost "fall into" the habit. Consider the examples of putting your alarm clock on top of your running gear for the morning; leaving the article you want to read across your computer keyboard; or attaching a Post-It note to your car keys to remind you to thank someone at the end of each day.

A third way you can also create a cue is by trying a *when/then* statement to prime your brain to spark the desired behavior in particular situations. For example: *when* I go to the restaurant, *then* I will order the healthy salad; *when* I get to work, *then* I will spend ten minutes checking in with a colleague; or *when* I eat my lunch, *then* I will research one new idea.[6]

You can combine all of these approaches to create super-charged cues to get your habit started, or just use the one that works best for you. Just try to ensure that your cue—in addition to triggering your routine—also triggers a craving for the reward. You see, when your brain starts to associate cues with certain rewards, a subconscious craving emerges that starts the habit loop spinning. Cravings are what drive habits and make forming a new habit easier.[7] So, as the cue triggers your behavior, give yourself a moment to really anticipate and savor the reward that will follow to make your habit more automatic.

Building a Routine

Researchers continue to discover tested routines that are specifically tailored to help you improve each of the twenty-four character strengths. For example, *creativity* can be improved by challenging yourself to come up with new uses for everyday objects; *bravery* can be boosted by continually stepping outside your comfort-zone; and *gratitude* can be lifted by counting your blessings each night. Using Michelle's experience with working alongside thousands of people to help them develop their strengths in workplaces, we've put together some highly effective routines for developing character strengths at work, which you'll find in the Appendix of this book.

When your routine is complete, make sure you take the time to enjoy your reward. In our rush to get everything done, it can be easy to whizz right past this important step. Rewards are the secret to consolidating your habits because they trigger a cascade of dopamine, your "feel good" neurological reward chemical, which sets up a craving for more of this behavior. It also helps to accelerate the creation of those neural connections that you've been building.[8]

Giving a Reward

Rewards can range from experiences that cause pleasurable physical sensations—such as food or relaxation—to emotional payoffs, like the feelings of pride that accompany praise or self-congratulation. For example, you might treat yourself to a green smoothie, a relaxing massage, or a new book to read. Or you might tick your habit off the list, use social media to share your accomplishments with friends, or report what you've achieved to a coach. Just try to do something in order to ensure a rush of dopamine hits your brain and sets up the craving for repeating the habit again—preferably without chocolate or alcohol. Often we're not conscious of the cravings that drive our behaviors, so initially you may need to experiment with different rewards to see what works best for you.

Creating Strengths-Based Habits

Based on Michelle's experience, we believe that creating a daily eleven-minute strengths-development habit is the most effective way to apply this science and deliver on the pathways to create your strengths-fueled future. But why eleven minutes?

Life gets busy. Bosses are demanding. Projects need juggling. And families and friends are waiting. There just never seems to be enough time to fit everything in. But even on your busiest days, we bet that there are ten minutes somewhere that you're not using. Perhaps you're commuting to work, waiting for a meeting to start, or having a moment of procrastination to try to avoid the things you're dreading. So if you had the chance for just ten minutes each day to show up at work and do what you do best, wouldn't this be one action worth prioritizing?

Becoming frustrated that no matter how much she wanted to be developing her strengths, Michelle just never seemed to find the time to begin, so she decided to start seizing one ten-minute gap each day to practice developing her strengths. She quickly discovered that ten minutes was excuse-proof. No matter what was happening in Michelle's day, she could always find this time somewhere by either getting up a little earlier, squeezing it in at lunchtime, or doing it before she went to bed. However, after learning more about our neurological habit loops, Michelle realized that trying to just create strength routines wasn't the most effective way to create lasting changes.

Michelle's efforts to develop her strengths were far more successful when she used a cue and a reward as well, so she added an extra minute to create the *11-Minute Strength-Development Habit.*

You can apply the eleven-minute strength-development habit formula like this:

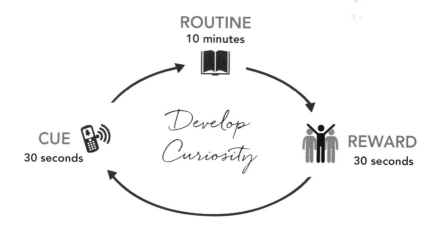

ROUTINE
10 minutes

Develop Curiosity

CUE
30 seconds

REWARD
30 seconds

To assist you in applying this formula, use the 11-Minute Strength-Development Habit play sheet to help turn your hope pathways into reality no matter how busy work or life gets.

Case In Point

By Michelle McQuaid

As an introvert who is dominated by the *wisdom* (head strengths) and *courage* (heart strengths) virtues, investing in relationships doesn't come easily to me. When leading teams, I always make sure my deputy is someone who excels in the *humanity* (strength of others) virtue to help round out my focus on tasks. This balance of our strengths makes us far more effective as a team.

Several years ago, when success at work increasingly relied upon your social capital, I decided it wasn't enough to just delegate my relationships. *Gratitude* was one of my top five strengths, and while I was fairly good at using it to appreciate the good things in my life, I realized that by focusing this strength toward others it might help improve my connections with them. To develop this strength, I decided to create a daily gratitude habit.

I cued up the gratitude habit in thirty seconds at the end of each day by anchoring it to my routine of packing up and getting ready to go home. I embedded the habit into my environment by placing a Post-It note on my car keys with the work "thank you" written on it to remind me. And to ensure the habit stuck, I used a when/then statement to prime my brain when I prepared my daily to-do list: when I get ready to go home, I will thank one person.

For the ten-minute routine, I decided to identify one person each day that had made my work a little easier or more enjoyable. I'd try to thank them face-to-face, but if they weren't around I'd do it with a phone call or an e-mail. Regardless of the medium, I always made sure to be specific about what I was thanking them for and why I appreciated it.

To reward myself in thirty seconds, I noted down whom I'd thanked, why I thanked them, and their reaction. This way I could watch the relationships I was investing in grow, I could savor the good things happening, and I could see the impact that this small habit was having on others and on myself. After I noted it down, I got the added bonus of going home. Both acts triggered the dopamine surge that helped me to start craving this use of my strengths the next time my cue was triggered.

I didn't tell anyone what I was doing. Although sometimes people were surprised they were being thanked—it wasn't a norm in our office culture—any awkwardness was quickly overcome when they realized I genuinely appreciated their efforts. After a week of practicing my new habit, I noticed I was walking out the door each night feeling a little lighter and happier.

What happened next though completely surprised me. This tidal wave of gratitude started rolling back toward me. Not just from people I thanked, but from people I hadn't even gotten to thanking yet. I was being stopped in the corridor and commended for my work. E-mails were arriving noting my support of other colleagues, and phone calls were being made appreciating the changes I was driving in the firm. My confidence, energy, and social capital soared on all this feedback.

What I hadn't understood when I created my habit is that when it comes to gratitude, we have a mindless, automatic reciprocation reflex. When someone shows us appreciation, we naturally want to respond in kind even if we don't act immediately. The result is an upward spiral of growth in our relationships that builds feelings of warmth and trust.

Although I'd never describe myself as a "people person," the development of my gratitude strength toward others softened my hard edges and made me far more approachable, so my professional and personal networks started to flourish. Using my strengths to do what I do best in just eleven minutes of cue, routine, and reward was all it took.

The 11-Minute Strength-Development Habit Play Sheet

Use this play sheet to create a daily eleven-minute strength-development habit to realize the pathways you selected on your Hope Map. Start with one habit, and when this is working well and becoming an automatic part of what you do each day, add the next habit, and then the next. You can keep adding strengths habits as long as they are guiding you and not governing you. Remember, each one is a gift of eleven minutes to just immerse yourself in doing what you do best.

The amount of time it takes for a habit to stick will vary depending on the type of person you are and the changes you're trying to make. Despite the popular myth that it takes twenty-one days to build a habit, recent studies suggest this can be anywhere between eighteen days to 254 days.[9] So be sure to tune in to how easy, effective, and joyful you're finding the habit, until the very idea of going a day without it makes you feel like you'd be missing out. Remember, if your habit is not sticking, play with the cue and the reward to make it easy to create a greater craving.

Try to start this habit within the next twenty-four to forty-eight hours so you don't lose your motivation for the change you want to experience.

1. **Identify the strengths you want to develop.** Determine which strength or cluster of strengths you want to focus on developing your golden mean for, based on one of the pathways in your Hope Map. You might be dialing up an underplayed strength, dialing down an overplayed strength, or simply being more consistent and frequent in a strength you've been using well.

2. **Cue the habit in thirty seconds.** Make it easy to get your strengths-development habit started by anchoring it to a habit you already have (like getting out of bed each morning, traveling to work, or turning on your computer), embedding it in your environment (such as putting your alarm clock on top of your running gear, leaving the article you want to read across your computer keyboard, or attaching a Post-It note reminder to your car keys), or using a *when/then* statement to prime your brain for specific situations (like, "*When* I get to work, *then* I will spend ten minutes checking in with a colleague"). Use one

The 11-Minute Strength-Development Habit Play Sheet

or more of these strategies to trigger the desired behavior, and take a moment to conjure up the reward waiting at the end of your routine to kick in the cravings that drive your habit loop.

3. **Practice your strengths-development routine for ten minutes.** Immerse yourself in a routine that will allow you to develop the golden mean of your chosen strengths. To help you think of routines that you can create to develop your strengths, look in the Appendix for ideas.

4. **Reward your behavior for thirty seconds.** Think of a physical (such as a green smoothie, a relaxing massage, or a nap) or emotional (like ticking your habit off the list, using social media to share your accomplishments with friends, or reporting what you've done to a coach) reward that will spark the natural flow of dopamine through your brain. It's preferable that you do this without chocolate or alcohol. Often we're not conscious of the cravings that drive our behaviors, so initially you may need to experiment with different rewards to see what works best for you.

You'll find it easier to follow through on your strength-development habit if you implement it around the same time each day. Also, because your self-regulation muscles wear down over the course of the day as you have to regulate your choices, emotions, and behaviors, you'll find it easier to stick with your habit if you start it earlier rather than later. It will also unleash a host of positive emotions to create an upward spiral of confidence and happiness that will propel you into the rest of your day.

The trick here is to put your goal of developing your strengths on autopilot by successfully building habits the right way. Good habits shouldn't constrain you, they shouldn't constrict you, and they shouldn't be a burden in your life. Rather, the kind of strength-development habits we want you to create should guide you in a way that liberates your energy to do more of the things that you love.

If you can, put your first cue in place now, or at the first opportunity you have, to trigger the behavior in the next twenty-four to forty-eight hours.

Correcting Bad Habits

You may find that your workday is already full of habits, and not all of them are geared toward your strengths. If you want to replace an old habit with a new strength-development habit, keep the cue and reward that are already working for you and simply replace the routine.

For example, you might have an existing daily habit in which you overplay your strength of *social intelligence* as follows: When you get your morning cup of coffee (your cue), you indulge in some negative gossip about the latest office politics with one of your colleagues (your routine), and then reinforce your social currency by sharing this information with the next person you meet (the reward). Over time, you've developed a strong craving for this habit loop because you've discovered that being a source of information makes you powerful. But negatively gossiping about people is a double-edged sword: it comes at a price to you and others by creating a downward spiral of negativity for everyone involved.[10] It's a very bad workplace habit.

You can change the habit and achieve a more positive result by keeping the cue (getting your morning coffee) and holding onto the reward you're craving (social currency from sharing information with others), but replacing your strength-development routine. Instead of using your strength of social intelligence to indulge in negative gossip, try highlighting people's positive qualities and good fortunes over their weaknesses and mishaps. Rather than stabbing people in the back, praise them behind their back and notice the positive impact it has on colleagues around you in terms of trust, confidence, and performance.[11]

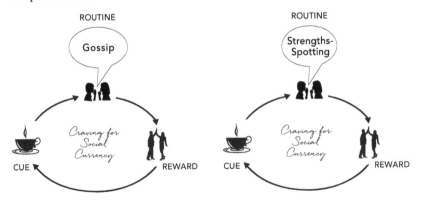

The formula remains the same—cue, routine, reward. You're simply replacing the routine that is holding you back with a strengths-development routine that propels you forward to the future you want. Researchers suggest that the hardest part of permanently making this shift in the existing habit loop is the belief that change is possible. Fostering the belief that things will get better is often easier in a community of people who are also making changes. Therefore, creating a "No Negative Gossip" pledge in your team is likely to make shifting this habit loop more successful.[12] As Gandhi once remarked, "As human beings our greatness lies not so much in being able to remake the world as in being able to remake ourselves."

Matching Your Work to Your Strengths

Unfortunately, most job descriptions—even when we work for ourselves—are not primarily written around our strengths. As a result, we often find ourselves running around meeting other people's expectations, and it feels like there's never enough time to really develop our strengths. But what if you paused for a moment, took a step back, and found ways to fuse your hopes and habits into what's already required in your work?

The science of job-crafting—the physical and cognitive changes individuals make in the task or relational boundaries of their work—is being used by a growing number of employees in a range of industries from executive leaders to entry-level roles. If you've ever taken a different approach to a task you were responsible for, changed a pattern of interaction with a client or a colleague, or refined how you thought about your job, then you've already started practicing this job-crafting strategy.[13]

Professor Amy Wrzesniewski at Yale University suggests that the best way to do this is to take a few minutes to analyze your job as you currently execute it by paying particularly close attention to how you are spending your time in the tasks and interactions that make up your work. Be sure to capture the activities and people that tend to consume your time and energy each day. Then divide them into those you enjoy and those you feel drained by.[14]

The activities you enjoy are usually a good indication of where your strengths already lie. Can you spot which character strengths you're developing in these moments? Do they reflect the activities and people you identified earlier in your flow audit? How many of these already fuse with the strengths-fueled best-possible future self you imagined and the hope pathways you identified for moving forward? Do you already have small, daily strengths habits in these areas? In Michelle's experience, you're often using your strengths at work more than you think—so take the time to really explore what might already exist for you to build upon.

When you've done this, reflect on what you could do to grow more of those things that you enjoy doing which align to the pathways you're pursuing and the habits you may wish to create. You can do this by:

- Changing the type and number of tasks that you undertake (the "what" you do in your job). What can you delegate, outsource, or reprioritize so that it's not absorbing so much of your time? What can you introduce, expand, or volunteer for, to shift your job toward the things you want to legitimately spend more time on? Is there an eleven-minute strength-development habit that aligns with the pathways you've chosen that would make this shift easier?

- Who are you spending your time with, and how are you spending your time with them? It turns out that when it comes to your level of engagement and wellbeing, more importantly than what you do each day at work is *who* you converse with.[15] Can you try to spend less time around colleagues and clients that drain your energy, or put strategies in place to manage the way you interact with them? Are there other people—sponsors, mentors, coaches, colleagues, or clients—you'd like to engineer opportunities to learn from or work alongside, in order to spend more time in the company of people you find energizing? Is there an eleven-minute strength-development habit that aligns with the pathways to make meeting and spending time with these people easier?

- Can you rethink how you feel about some of the elements of your work? Is there a way to see activities or people you haven't been enjoying as lessons to be conquered, so you can move past them? To help you make some of the most mundane parts of your job more meaningful, turn a piece of paper horizontally and complete the following steps. First, on the left-hand side, write down a job task that feels devoid of meaning. Then ask, "What is the purpose of this task? What will I accomplish? Who does it help?" Draw an arrow to the right and write this answer down. If what's written still seems unimportant, ask once more, "What does this result lead to?" Draw another arrow and write it down. Keep working through this process until there's a result that is meaningful to you, so it's possible to see the sum of small tasks.[16] Could embedding this small task in an eleven-minute strength-development habit make it easier and more enjoyable?

Then, and perhaps most importantly, experiment with what's possible. You'll need to move past the stories you've created about how people "expect" you to spend your time and find small moments. Once again, your eleven-minute strength-development habits are the perfect tool to turn the job you have into a job you love. If you need more help figuring this out, then grab the job-crafting toolkit online at http://www.jobcrafting.org to guide you through these steps in more detail.

Studies have found that by customizing the design of our own jobs, we're better able to meet our needs for control over our work, develop positive self-images, and establish connections with others. It also helps us to make our work more meaningful, to better juggle what's being demanded of us with the resources we have available, and to feel more engaged and less absent from our jobs. Not only do job crafters experience higher levels of happiness and wellbeing, but their performance is also better. Evidence suggests that these benefits extend beyond the employee themselves and out through the organization.[17]

Case In Point

By Michelle McQuaid

Belinda was the general manager of a small and quickly growing company that provided professional development to owner-operated businesses. She loved her job because she honestly believed that what she did somehow mattered. Most of their clients were mom-and-pop businesses—the backbone of local economies—and Belinda enjoyed finding ways to help them *do well* financially and *do good* in the community.

When Belinda came to me for coaching, however, it was because all the joy had gone out of her job. Her boss, the sole owner of the company, increasingly seemed more interested in making money to fill his own pockets than to invest any of it in the strategies Belinda was recommending to better support their clients. When more than five-hundred-thousand dollars earmarked for future development disappeared from the company account, he urged Belinda to use it as a learning opportunity to be more innovative in her thinking and practices. Demoralized by her boss's greed and selfishness, Belinda found herself in a vicious downward spiral of disappointment, despair, and helplessness that was impacting her work and her life.

With the character strengths of *social intelligence, kindness, curiosity, leadership,* and *creativity*, Belinda discovered her best moments involved meeting and helping others by understanding their needs and finding new ways to help meet them. She loved coaching people to success. Doing more of this work each day was what filled her strengths-fueled vision of the future and the hope pathways she mapped out. But how would she fit this in with all her current responsibilities?

Rather than adding one more thing to her list of daily tasks, we stepped back to look at where Belinda's time, energy, and attention was currently devoted. It didn't take long for us to see that it wasn't *what* she was doing each day at work that was draining her energy, but who she was doing some of it with, as well as the beliefs she'd come to hold about the purpose of her work.

When it came to *what* she was doing, Belinda could see that each coaching moment, not just with her clients but also her team members, was an opportunity to develop her social *intelligence, kindness,* and *curiosity* strengths. So, she developed the following eleven-minute habit: "When I arrive at work each morning, then I'll take ten minutes to check in with a team member to see how they're doing before getting my morning coffee." For the rest of her job (those tasks not focused on the development of others), Belinda looked for ways to delegate, outsource, or reprioritize them. This gave her more time in her day, legitimately aligned to her job responsibilities, to find ways to coach others.

When it came to *who* she was doing her work with, Belinda realized that spending time with her boss left her feeling completely disillusioned, but spending time with her clients left her feeling inspired and appreciated. Wanting to use her strengths of *curiosity* and *creativity* to meet the innovation expectations of her job, Belinda's second eleven-minute habit was: "When I finish my lunch, then I'll call one client and ask what could be done to better support them, and add their ideas to my list of innovative 'aha' moments." To avoid having to spend too much time with her boss, Belinda also started booking more meetings out of the office with clients, and getting closer to the coalface of their business. She also sought out a handful of mentors outside of her company to give her the development support she craved but wasn't getting at work.

When it came to *why* she did her job, Belinda wanted to reconnect to the original sense of meaning and purpose she found in helping her clients do well and do good in the world. Hoping to be the kind of leader she wished she had, Belinda's third eleven-minute habit was to use her strength of *leadership* so that when she opened her diary each morning, she would pause to reflect on how the work she and her team were prioritizing that day could help the mom-and-pop businesses flourish. Her reward was to be able to start doing the work. Each day, this habit helped Belinda focus on why her work mattered, allowing her to distance herself from the money-hungry urges of her boss.

Not only did these small habits start to make Belinda's day more enjoyable, and help her to focus her attention on what was within her control, it created an upward spiral of confidence, hope, and growth that made her far more effective at work. The coaching role she took with the team meant they were soon stepping up to take on the more mundane tasks she'd been carrying. The innovation calls with clients were surfacing ideas that both she and her boss were excited to implement (although their motivations remained divided). By spending more time in the company of clients and mentors who inspired her, she felt more respected, valued, and appreciated in her work. Nine months later, she was headhunted for a role that aligned her sense of purpose and the daily development of her strengths, with a much nicer boss.

Building Grit to Create Lasting Changes

Now you've discovered your strengths, dreamed of what's possible, designed the pathways to move you forward, and are ready to deliver the small changes that will make developing your strengths each day at work possible. But will your efforts last? Creating lasting change in our lives isn't easy, not least because we have a built-in tendency to adapt, particularly to the good things in our life.

Scientists call this phenomenon "hedonic adaptation," and while the rate to which we adapt varies between people and situations, the creeping toll of normalcy and our ever-increasing expectations are a normal part of human functioning. It's why a strength-development habit that initially brings you so much joy can start to feel boring and tedious as time goes by. The good news is that researchers have found that it's possible to train our brains to overcome, forestall, or at least slow down hedonic adaptation by being grateful for the rewards our habits bring, keeping our habits novel by mixing them up, comprehending the significance of our chosen habits, and not comparing ourselves to others.[18]

The truth is, you'll need to find ways to head off adaptation if you want to create the strengths-fueled future you've dreamed of. You see, studies have found that there is one quality shared by the leaders in every field—a quality that gives them the stamina to live their life as though it's a marathon and not a sprint. That quality is *grit*.

Associate Professor Angela Duckworth at the University of Pennsylvania set out to explore what distinguished star performers in law, journalism, investment banking, painting, academia, and medicine. What she discovered is that these individuals cited "grit," or a close synonym, as a talent. In fact, many of the people she interviewed were awed by the achievements of peers who did not at first seem as gifted as others, but whose sustained commitment to their ambitions was exceptional. Likewise, many noted with surprise that prodigiously gifted peers did not end up in the upper echelons of their field. It seems that gritty individuals approach the journey to mastery like a marathon rather than a sprint, and this fuels their stamina to practice their talent over and over again.[19]

Duckworth defines "grit" as the tendency to sustain interest in and effort toward very long-term goals. It entails working consistently toward challenges and being able to maintain interest and effort over the years despite failures, setbacks, and plateaus in progress. Whereas most of us take disappointment or boredom as signals that it's time to change our approach and cut our losses, people with grit take these signs as the moment when they need to stick with it and truly show up. Her research has established the predictive power of grit, over and beyond measures of talent, for objectively measured success outcomes.[20]

While much is still being learned about grit, when it comes to realizing your strengths-fueled best-possible future self by pursuing your chosen pathways and sticking to your habits, Duckworth suggests four things you can do to improve your levels of grit:

- **Be meaningfully interested.** Make sure your long-term goal is set around something that is interesting and meaningful to you. The magic of grit happens when you have both. For example, you might be interested in ice cream, but do you really find it meaningful and want to be gritty in your pursuit of it? Professor William Damon at Stanford University has found that when we find something personally interesting and meaningful to the world beyond ourselves, we're able to connect passion with action, to provide a sense of purpose and energy that prevents burnout and promotes resiliency.[21] Because your strengths-fueled best-possible future self was grounded in purpose-focused "want-to" goals, it should already meet this requirement. But if you skimmed or skipped this step, it's worth revisiting Chapter 4 now.

- **Cultivate growth mindsets.** Studies find that grit is positively correlated with the belief that we can improve our talents and abilities. Having a "growth mindset" is one of the cognitive antecedents that makes you more inclined to be gritty because it cultivates the belief that things can improve, that failure is not permanent, and that there is a reason to persist.[22] We explored ways to tune in and cultivate your growth mindset when you set down you Hope Map. But if you skimmed or skipped this step, it's worth revisiting Chapter 5 now.

- **Invest in deliberate practice.** Professor Anders Ericsson's studies of world-class experts across different fields have found that one of the primary things that sets these experts apart is that they practice the development of their strengths in specific ways. The deliberate practice they undertake meets the following requirements when it comes to improving their skills: setting specific goals for micro-improvements, chasing a level of challenge that exceeds their current level of skills (focus on doing things they can't yet do), seeking immediate and informative feedback, and practicing until the point of mastery is reached and they can perform on autopilot.[23] The strengths-development habits we've focused on in this chapter are a great way to invest in deliberate practice. However, you can apply Ericsson's steps if you want to stretch your strengths mastery even further.

- **Ask for support.** Rely on other people around you to hold you accountable to your goals and ensure you don't quit in the face of boredom, frustration, or discouragement. A common feature in the stories of top performers is that there were times where they stumbled and there were times when they doubted themselves. It wasn't all easy for them, and in many cases, they relied on someone else, not themselves.[24] When you identified ways to maintain your will power on your Hope Map, we encouraged you to identify the people who can help support your journey. If you skimmed or missed this step, revisit your Hope Map (page 120) now and be sure to add the people who will keep you accountable and urge you on when you're tempted to give up.

As Woody Allen once noted, "Eighty percent of success in life is showing up." While Duckworth suggests that there is nothing magic about the number 'eighty percent', she does agree that for many endeavors, you'll overcome most of the challenges you face on the way to reaching your goals if you persist and keep showing up.[25] As we've guided you through each step of our strengths-development blueprint, we've tried to help you ignite and embed elements to build your grit so you can achieve your strengths-fueled future and truly show up, shine, and succeed in ways you're proud of at work. Now you just have to start.

PART C
Building on Your Strengths

7. Where Can You Embed Your Strengths at Work?

Ensuring Your Strengths Are Valued

Setting Your Performance Goals

Preparing for Performance Reviews

Giving Feedback

Spotting Strengths in Others

Creating Micro-Moments of Connection

Finding the Best in Others

Improving Your Relationships

Becoming a Strengths-Led Organization

Recruiting for Strengths

Investing in the Development of Strengths

Providing Strengths Feedback

CHAPTER 7

Where Can You Embed Your Strengths at Work?

Now that you understand the potential benefits of developing your strengths, and you're looking forward to making your strengths-fueled future a reality, you might be feeling a little bit nervous about how other people at work are going to respond to the changes you want to be creating. Remember, our brains are hard-wired to focus on spotting and fixing weaknesses. Although there is sound scientific evidence supporting the approach you want to take, people unaware of this research and these practices may feel that your new ideas are counterintuitive.

Unfortunately, many organizations, their leaders, and the management systems and processes they create remain oblivious to the power of strengths-based leadership when it comes to engaging, developing, and rewarding their people. And even when you're the boss, the idea that you're going to prioritize developing strengths rather than fixing weaknesses can feel unsettling and revolutionary to the people you're leading.

In this chapter, we'll help you embed your strengths so they become a way of life in your work no matter what your role is, or what your organization's current appetite for strengths-based approaches might be. We'll show you how to help your boss recognize, develop, and reward your strengths, even if he/she has no idea what your strengths are. We'll also show you how to build better relationships—even with your most difficult colleagues—by seeing and valuing the strengths in others. Again, these are small changes that can make a positive difference in your results. You won't need anyone's permission, a budget, or a team to execute them. All you need is the knowledge, tools, and willingness to act.

And if your organization is ready to take it to the next level, we'll leave you with the simple people-management processes for strengths-based recruitment, performance management, and feedback, which Michelle has successfully applied in companies. These approaches aim to make the prioritization and development of strengths an organizational strategy to help you to outperform your competitors. In other words, these approaches will ensure that consistently bringing out the best in your people becomes a way of organizational life.

Ensuring Your Strengths are Valued

Developing your strengths should be a win for you, a win for your team, and a win for your organization. We've seen that evidence suggests that when you use your strengths regularly at work, you're more engaged, and as a result, you can help your team to be more productive and your organization to have customers who are more satisfied. But to actually achieve this, you'll need to ensure your developing your strengths in ways that align with your organization's business strategy.

Setting Your Performance Goals

One of the ways many organizations try to ensure that what you do each day will help them achieve their overall objectives is to meet with your boss and agree on a set of personal goals about what you will achieve in the year ahead. These are generally recorded in what's called a performance or development plan. This is used to review your ability to deliver value to the organization, to give you feedback, and to determine any rewards such as bonuses, pay raises, or promotions at the end of the year.

Unfortunately, in most organizations, few of these conversations or planning templates focus on your strengths. As a result, many bosses and employees think of this exercise as just another corporate compliance requirement they want to complete as quickly as possible. But no matter how much your boss understands the value of strengths leadership, this is a pivotal moment for you to align the next year of your working life to the strengths-development opportunities you're craving.

Before you sit down to complete the company-issued templates or have a goal-setting conversation with your boss, take the time to:

- **Understand what you want.** Review your strengths-fueled best-possible future self and your Hope Map. What does success look like to you, and what are the things you'd like to be doing to develop your strengths? Write down the support you'll need to make this a reality in terms of on-the-job learning opportunities, formal training, or coaching.

- **Understand what your company wants.** Dig into the current business strategy for your organization. Even if your role feels a long way away from these lofty goals and broad pathways, remember that these are the hopes of your leaders. Can you find synergies with your own "want-to" goals or pathways? Write down any of these shared goals and activities.

  If the alignment is not obvious, try the job-crafting exercise in Chapter 6 to help you rethink your company's business strategy. Ask yourself, "What's the purpose of these corporate goals?" and "Who do they help?", until you can find the every-day relevance to the things you actually want to be doing in your work.

- **Recognize what your boss wants.** How do you think your boss is going when it comes to delivering their responsibilities for the business strategy? What is your boss hoping to achieve for the organization, your team, and for themselves in the year ahead? What goals have they shared, and which pathways are consuming their attention and resources? What opportunities does this open up for developing your strengths in the ways you want? Again, try to find synergies between what your boss needs to get done and your "want-to" goals and hope pathways. Write these down.

Looking at the three lists you've now created—what you want, what your organization wants, and what your boss wants—can you find goals or pathways where all three overlap? You may need to use a little creative interpretation to find these links, as even the best-laid company plans often fail to link the organizational strategy to the priorities of their leaders.

It can help to jot down your observations on different-colored Post-It notes. Then, using an empty wall or your desk (probably not where your boss can see them), try to come up with groupings of like goals and pathways. For example, a blue Post-It with your goal may say, "help develop the best in others"; a green Post-It with your organization's goal may say, "unleash the potential of its people"; and a red Post-It with your boss's hope may say to "improve team productivity." These goals all share the aspiration to help employees perform better and could be grouped together as a win-win-win priority. It doesn't matter how many Post-It notes overlap in a group, but be sure to have at least one of each color so you're confident that you, your organization, and your boss are aligned.

Why does this matter? Your boss is unlikely to agree to a performance or development plan that only benefits your interests, regardless of whether using your strengths regularly is good for your wellbeing. They have a business responsibility to ensure that the activities you're committed to delivering will benefit the organization. It's also in your boss's professional and personal interests to make sure the things you're going to be doing will make them look good and make their life easier.

Most bosses will approach your annual performance and development plan top-down. They'll think about what the company is trying to achieve, which parts they are responsible for delivering, and then try to fit you in a box that best serves their needs. This is why so few of us have a chance to do what we do best each day at work.

The more effective approach when it comes to creating lasting, positive changes is to plan top-down, bottom-up, and then squeeze it from the sides.[1] You need to understand the top-down organizational wants, as this is what keeps you employed. You need to be clear on the bottom-up personal wants that make your work engaging, effective, and enjoyable. And you need to recognize the side-squeeze that comes from your boss's wants, as this will shape and support your developmental opportunities, and significantly influence your evaluation and rewards.

Too few organizations have the insight and rigor in performance and development-planning conversations to do this for you. You need to do this for yourself. This is a year of your life you won't get to live over.

Once you have a clear sense of what the win-win-win performance and development plan might look like in the year ahead, then you're ready to sit down and complete the necessary company-issued templates and have the conversation with your boss. Remember, positive images will pull you forward and help you see opportunities that might otherwise be missed.

If the templates that your organization provides you with don't prompt you to name your strengths and ways to develop them, simply add them in regardless. For example, if the template asks you to:

- **"List the performance goals you will achieve this year that are specific to your role."** You could write something like, "I'll use my strengths of teamwork and curiosity to find innovative ways we can use technology to bring out the best in each other, improve our productivity as a team, and unleash our potential."

- **"Identify the development goals you would like support in achieving this year to improve your knowledge and skills."** You could write something like, "I'd like to develop my strength of social intelligence through formal training in a social-emotional intelligence program so I can better cultivate more supportive and productive relationships with my colleagues and clients."

By naming your strengths, even when the template doesn't ask for them, you're making it easy for your boss to gain insight into when you're at your best. By linking the organizational strategy and your boss's priorities to the activities you'd like to focus on to help develop your strengths, you're making it easier for them to see the win-win-win benefits and agree to the performance and development plan that moves you toward the strengths-fueled future you want.

Of course, they may not agree to everything you've proposed, no matter how well it's written. But this preparation allows you to have a business-focused conversation with your boss about opportunities for developing your strengths, and genuinely explore ways to match these opportunities to your job. And if your boss agrees to none of it, remember that you've already found a way to do what you do best for at least eleven minutes a day.

Preparing for Performance Reviews

The other end of this performance cycle usually arrives twelve months later when your performance is reviewed. Again, there is often a template to complete, and a conversation with your boss where you demonstrate how you performed and the progress you've made on your original goals. To do this, you're required to present an evidence-base of key metrics you've secured like customer satisfaction scores, sales numbers, or costs you've saved, and any feedback you can collect from your clients, colleagues, and other stakeholders.

With the promise of more money and promotions hanging in the balance, most of us spend a little more time on this part of the compliance process. However, when it comes to the evidence we provide, we also have a tendency to only color within the lines of what the company-provided templates or our bosses prompt us for. Although it's our natural inclination to look for the things we do well, our haste to grab on to any good result means we often miss the opportunity to further educate our boss and organization about the strengths—the things we do well and enjoy doing—we want to be valued for.

If the company-provided templates don't prompt you for your strengths and the ways you've developed them over the year, simply add them in regardless. For example, if the template asks you to:

- **"Demonstrate how you've delivered your performance goals for this period."** You could write something like, "I've used my strengths of teamwork and curiosity to find innovative new ways we can use technology, like introducing Yammer to keep us connected on projects, so we've been able to consistently support and encourage each other no matter where we're physically located. This has helped us improve our productivity as a team, with members noting it has saved significant time in getting feedback, which enables us to implement solutions more quickly and deliver ahead of deadlines on numerous projects. It has also helped unleash our potential by allowing us to co-create new ideas in real-time for problems our clients have been unable to solve."

- **"Provide feedback from key stakeholders on the contributions you've made to help achieve your team and our organizational objectives."** As you collect this feedback from stakeholders, share what strengths you've been trying to develop, and ask them to note ways you've applied them and how this has been valuable. You could say, "I'd be most grateful for any feedback you can provide on my performance in this role over the last twelve months. I've particularly been working on developing my strengths of teamwork and curiosity when it comes to how we're using technology to collaborate. If you've found these strengths of value in my work, please provide an example and how it helped you and/or others."

- **"Identify areas of improvement."** Try to focus this on how you've developed your strengths—be it dialing them up or dialing them down—to find your golden mean in different situations. You could write, "I dialed down my strength of zest at the start of new projects to ensure we had the commitment of key stakeholders before we got started. I dialed up my strength of social intelligence to better tune in to my client's motivations to ensure that the solutions we were creating truly met their needs."

Unfortunately, most bosses are still not taught how to give strengths-development feedback, so you should be prepared to help guide the conversation toward the insights that will serve you best. For example:

- **If your boss details examples where you've failed to meet your performance goals**, be sure to ask something like, "I hear your concerns and will think about ways I can improve upon the issues raised. Can you help me put your feedback into the context of all the effort I've made this year about what was working?"

Alternative strengths prompting feedback questions may include, "I understand my performance on that project was not what you hoped for. Can you give me one example of my work this year you've been happiest with?" Or, "I understand not everything I tried this year went the way we both wanted. Overall though, what percentage of my performance do you think is working well?"

When it comes to reviewing your performance, it's natural for a boss to fixate on all the things you've done wrong—this is their negativity bias in action. When hearing this negative feedback, it's easy to hit a downward spiral of despair and walk away from the conversation feeling as if all your effort was wasted. By asking your boss to provide examples of work they are happy with, it helps to balance their urge to spot weaknesses with their ability to notice your strengths and ways to build upon them.

- **If your boss is intent on detailing weaknesses that they believe need work** when it comes to your areas of development, try saying, "It's clear that I need to slow down on projects in areas you'd like me to improve. Do you think this could be my strength of zest being overplayed?" Or, "Do you think I could dial-up or dial-down a strength to improve this area?"

Remember, it will be your boss's natural inclination to point out weaknesses they believe need to be fixed. You can help your boss become more strengths-savvy by prompting them to look more broadly, guiding them toward strengths-development solutions that will deliver the results you both want.

Giving Feedback

As part of the annual review process, you should apply the same principles when you provide feedback on your boss or colleagues' performance. Think about the strengths you've seen them using when they're most engaged, energized, and enjoying their work. When you reflect on what they've done well, try to name their strengths and how they've applied them in ways you value. Equally, if there are areas for improvement, try to be specific about the strengths you think they could dial up or dial down to get a better result.

These small shifts can be made regardless of the official people-management processes or systems that exist in your organization. By choosing to prioritize strengths when it comes to the development and performance of people at your work, you create a moment of inflection that paves the way for people to start looking at you, themselves, and others through the lens of buildable strengths. It helps to plant the seed of change you want to create in your organization, which can grow in ways you've never imagined. As Gandhi famously suggested, "Be the change you want to see."

Spotting Strengths in Others

Dr. George Vaillant is famous for running one of the longest psychological studies of all time, called the Harvard Grant Study. Every two years across a seventy-year period, the Harvard Grant Study evaluated Harvard sophomores and disadvantaged inner-city youth on their mental and physical health, career enjoyment, and their relationships. Vaillant sums up everything they've learned like this: "Seventy years of evidence proved one very important thing. Our relationships with other people matter and matter more than anything else in the world."[2]

Other studies have found that each positive interaction you have during the course of a work day actually helps return your cardiovascular system back to resting levels, and over the long haul, they protect you from the negative effects of job strain.[3] If you have a best friend at work, you are seven times more likely to be engaged in your job, as well as to engage customers, produce higher quality work, and improve your wellbeing. Furthermore, it's also less likely that you'll be injured on the job.[4]

Why do our relationships matter so much at work? The truth is, you have a biological need for social support, and every time you get to genuinely connect with another person, the pleasure-inducing hormone oxytocin is released into your bloodstream. This helps to reduce your anxiety, and improve your concentration and focus. [5]

Creating Micro-Moments of Connection

Luckily, Professor Barbara Fredrickson at the University of North Carolina has discovered that it takes just a micro-moment of genuine connection to spark an upward spiral of mutual care between people. Her research suggests it takes three simple steps:

- The sharing of a positive emotion, such as interest, joy, amusement, or pride.

- The synchronization of your biochemistry and behaviors through shared eye contact, or matching your body gestures or vocal tone.

- A reflective motive to invest in each other's wellbeing that brings about feelings of warmth and trust.

Fredrickson describes this process as "positivity resonance" and suggests that you think of it like a mirror. You and the other person mirror the positivity in each other's emotional state. You mirror each other's body and brain activity. And you mirror each other's impulse to care for one another. In these moments, you each become the reflection and extension of each other, truly making two heads better than one.

Not only that, but when you experience warm and trusting feelings toward another person, it improves your vagal tone. This is the very subtle arrhythmia that occurs with each breath you take. It helps to calm down your naturally high heart rate, regulate glucose and cardiovascular health, regulate your attention and emotion at work, and helps you have better social skills.[6]

Investing in micro-moments of connection can help to meet the deep, psychological need we all share to be respected, valued, and appreciated. As William James once observed, "the deepest principle in human nature is the craving to be appreciated." One of the easiest ways to meet this need in others and create a micro-moment of connection is to look for people's strengths and tell them what you see.

Think about it. When was the last time you walked into a meeting with your colleagues with the intention of looking for the best in them? If you're like most of us, it's not often. But how would you feel working alongside people whom you knew respected, valued, and appreciated the strengths you brought into each interaction? How would this enable you to function at work? What might you be able to achieve?

The good news is, once you know what you're looking for, spotting strengths in others is simple. Just like you, when people are using their strengths, they light up and come alive. Their pupils might widen. Their body movements become more active. Their speed and tone of speech generally lifts. When you see a colleague's eyes sparkling, their hands gesturing to make a point or share an idea, or their voice is quick and animated, you know their strengths are at work. They're clearly more engaged, energized, and enjoying what they're doing.[7] The hardest part is just remembering to look.

Finding the Best in Others

Once you start hunting for the best in others, it helps to name or label what you're seeing. The twenty-four VIA character strengths offer a ready-made vocabulary of researched insights to help organize your observations. But trying to remember all the strengths can be challenging, so one of the shortcuts Michelle often teaches are the six VIA virtue categories. Remember, each of the character strengths falls within one of the following virtue categories—take another look at the table on the Spotting Strengths play sheet to remind you.

- **Head Strengths**—Someone who has a high *wisdom* virtue is normally telling you about their latest new ideas, sharing a great piece of research they've just discovered, challenging your mind with new possibilities, or urging you to look at the bigger picture and weigh up different perspectives. These are cognitive strengths that involve the acquisition and use of knowledge. Albert Einstein is an example of someone whose head strengths were in action.

- **Heart Strengths**—Someone who has a high *courage* virtue puts his/her heart on the line. These people are willing to take risks, will persevere no matter how difficult things get, will always tell it like it is, and have a certain amount of energy and vitality around what they're doing. These are emotional strengths that involve the exercise of will to accomplish goals in the face of internal or external opposition. Nelson Mandela's heart strengths made change possible.

- **Strengths of Others**—Someone who has a high *humanity* virtue is often going out of his/her way to take care of others. These are people renowned for their thoughtfulness, who take the time to listen and understand what others need, who perform acts of kindness unprompted, and who are comfortable with people's emotion. This is particularly true one-on-one. These are interpersonal strengths that entail "tending and befriending" others. Princess Diana used her humanity strengths to connect with individuals through her charity work, and this was the reason she earned the moniker "Queen of Hearts."

- **Strengths of Self**—Someone who has a high *temperance* virtue is generally recognized for his/her high levels of self-control and managing the ways they show up. These people are able to regulate their choices, emotions, and behaviors, are quick to forgive and don't seek punishment of others, deliver the plan no matter what challenges they encounter, and are often happiest out of the spotlight where they can get on with what needs to be done. These are strengths that protect against excess. Gandhi's ability to manage his thoughts, emotions, and behaviors to undertake only the most calculated risks, while wishing he had never been named Mahatma (revered person), is a fine example of what the strengths of self look like.

- **Strengths of Community**—Someone who has a high *justice* virtue values his/her community and wants to do right by others. These people make sure everybody on the team gets a fair go, they organize others to make things happen, or willingly support the team to make the whole stronger than the parts. These are civic strengths that underlie healthy community life. When Martin Luther King declared that he wanted "freedom for all men," his justice strengths were displayed to the world.

- **Strengths of Spirit**—Someone who has a high *transcendence* virtue lifts you up whenever you spend time with them. These people inspire others with meaning—giving them hope, making them laugh, and appreciating them. They connect us to what is true, good, and possible in the physical, mental, and spiritual world around us. These are strengths that build connection to a larger universe and provide meaning. Comedian Robin Williams was an example of this virtue in action. Not only did he make us laugh, but through the various mediums of his work and the way he lived his life, he lifted up the spirits of everyone around him.

Imagine using these virtue categories to spot strengths just like you would use a camera to take a casual snap shot of someone at their best. It's a momentary image of how the person appears to you. As you become more confident and capable at strength spotting—just like a good photographer—we urge you to take the time to notice the finer details in the image of the specific character strengths you see showing up, and pay attention to whether these are replicated across other snapshots.

As you reflected on some of the famous examples cited above, you may have wondered if someone can have more than one strength virtue. Albert Einstein demonstrated many of the head strengths, but what about his sense of *humor* and *playfulness*, his *hope*, and his love of music? Many of us find that our character strengths cluster under more than just one virtue, as discussed in Chapter 3. You may have discovered you were dominant in two particular virtues with a couple of character strengths appearing in each. Or you may even have found that you had one strength under almost every virtue.

This is why the goal in spotting strengths is not to put people in a nicely labeled box and then assume you know everything about them. Rather, your goal is to start looking for where they're at their best and see if you can find the patterns repeatedly appearing. For some people, no matter what situation you see them in, the same virtue group will appear again and again. For other people, it may seem that different strengths are surfacing every time you see them. Be content to embrace the wonderful complexity of human life and know that your job is simply to appreciate what you're seeing.

Michelle often finds that after completing the VIA Survey, people ask their colleagues and clients if they'd be interested in using the tool and sharing their results to find the best ways of working together. Most of us are curious about what we look like at our best, so this is rarely a hard sell.

In sharing your results, be sure you take the time to understand how your colleagues like to develop their top strengths at work. For example, just because you both share creativity as a signature strength, it doesn't mean you'll enjoy developing it in the same way. One of you might love mind-mapping ideas, while the other person would prefer to be prototyping. Use the questions from the play sheet in Chapter 3 (page 81) to help you discover the golden mean of each other's strengths.

Improving Your Relationships

As you become more confident in the patterns you're seeing, or people have shared their VIA Survey results with you directly, you can begin to use this information to create more micro-moments of connection. Remember, character strengths are things we value in their own right. They intrinsically motivate us to act because of the moral beliefs we hold, even if we're not paid or recognized for these particular choices. As a result, understanding people's dominant strengths provides an interesting window of insight into how you can improve your working relationships with each other. For example:

- **Resourcing and valuing strengths:** Next time you need someone to help get something done, take a moment to think about whose strengths are most suited to the tasks. For example, someone who is high in the strength of *kindness* will naturally prioritize creating a caring, supportive environment for your next team day. And someone who is high in the strength of *love of learning* will want to really dig into the research to shape future strategies. Not only will they be energized by the task you've asked them to take on, but they're likely to be far more effective as well.

- **Tailoring strengths communication:** Before you write the next e-mail, make the next phone call, or prepare the next presentation, take a moment to think about the strengths of your audience and what is most likely to motivate them to act. For example, if you wanted your boss who is high in the strength of *love* to sign off on a project, then you might focus on the human stories that demonstrate the benefits of proceeding. On the other hand, if you wanted a boss who has a high strength of *curiosity* to sign off the same project, then you might focus on statistics and facts to demonstrate the benefits of going ahead. Both benefits are real. Both benefits may be part of your presentation. But the emphasis you present on different information could be tailored to your boss's intrinsic motivations in order to improve the chances of the project being signed off.

- **Personalizing strength connections:** Team-building activities and client entertaining are common business approaches to getting to know more about each other. But before you send out the next invitation, consider what will appeal to this person's strengths so you can get to know the best about them. For example, if you have a client who is high in the strength of humor, you might invite them as your guest to a funny play or a comedy act. On the other hand, if you have a client who is high in the strength of *fairness*, you might invite them as your guest to a fundraising activity for a non-profit organization.

- **Being mindful of strength collisions:** Every now and then, we each encounter someone we struggle spending time with. It's like you're oil and water and just shouldn't be mixed with each other. But before you start keeping a list about all the things they do that drive you mad, breathe and step back to see if you can spot how your strengths might be colliding. For example, if you have a colleague who is single-minded in their determination to get things done, this may be their strength of *perseverance* in action. If you are high in the strength of humor and feel you have no permission to have some fun as you go about your work with them, then it's easy to see how your strengths may be colliding. Chances are, you're finding them boring and they're finding you undisciplined.

By recognizing that you have different character strengths—different values in play—it's possible to de-personalize the tension you're feeling and create a bridge of empathy and respect to solve your differences. Think of it like this: your colleague isn't being boring to deliberately make your day miserable; they're just at their best when focusing on a task. By respecting, valuing, and appreciating this about them, you can also explain that you're at your best when you can have a little fun while you work. Then ask if there is a way you can balance both your strengths—like a regular five-minute humor break— so you can finish the job more effectively, quickly, and enjoyably together. You may not become best friends, but you will remove unnecessary stress from your relationship.

The goal is not to manipulate your relationships, but to genuinely understand what interests people and how you can connect around shared values as a means of accelerating trust. In the words of William Arthur Ward, "When we seek to bring out the best in others, we somehow bring out the best in ourselves."

Case In Point

By Michelle McQuaid

I thought my new boss was a stick in the mud. She was boring, unwilling to take risks, and paid a crazy level of attention to the smallest details on the project I was responsible for delivering. I dreaded her meetings and had started doing all I could to avoid having to spend time with her.

Mind you, I don't think she thought that highly of me either. I had the distinct impression she saw me as irresponsible when it came to spending company resources, flighty when it came to following through on ideas, and more interested in enjoying my work than doing what had to be done. Put it this way—her face tended to cloud over rather than light up when I walked into her office.

Needless to say, this made working together reasonably challenging. My stress levels went up with each encounter, as ideas were squashed and milestones rigidly adhered to. This was not how I worked at my best, and in an effort to stay focused on the big picture of my career and not become overwhelmed with feelings of helplessness and despair, I'd resorted to counting the days until this project would be over.

As a result, I'd stopped doing my best work, and little by little things started to go wrong. Desperately in need of a new strategy, I decided to step back from our relationship and see if I could spot her strengths (trust me, they were the last things I felt like finding). When I did look, it became clear that at her best—those times when she lit up—my boss was minimizing risks, making sure deadlines stuck, and driving us through to deliver the project no matter what. It was her strength of *prudence*— her ability to be careful—that she was drawing on. She wasn't trying to be a frustrating, boring stick in the mud when it came to our work; she was just trying to do what she did best.

I found her approach so challenging because one of my top character strengths is *creativity*. I'm at my best when coming up with new ideas, being flexible in my approach as opportunities arise, and having fun as I create results. My boss's strength to rigorously follow the plan, and my strength for opportunistic creativity, were clearly colliding and leaving our working relationship fraught with difficulties.

By understanding the clash between our strengths, I was able to look at my boss's behavior with a newfound empathy. It seemed unlikely that she was behaving this way just to annoy me, and much more likely that she was just trying to do her best for the project. By believing that she wasn't trying to personally antagonize me, the sting was immediately removed from our encounters, and I was able to start viewing the things she did that drove me crazy as the strengths she offered to ensure our work was a success. Don't get me wrong, I still didn't love the way she acted, but I could respect, value, and appreciate the strengths she had that I lacked.

I also decided that we'd benefit from a conversation about how we could work better together. I explained that while I understood her strength of *prudence* was important to keep us accountable and on track, my strength was *creativity*, and we'd get a better result overall if there was space to responsibly apply this from time to time on the work we were doing. She agreed that while this wasn't her natural way of working, she could see that occasional moments of creative exploration wouldn't undermine—and may even improve—the outcomes we were chasing.

We didn't become best friends, and I was still glad when this particular project was done. But I did stop dreading those meetings with her, my stress levels returned to normal, and together we were able to deliver a better result than either of us could have done without the other's strengths. All it required was being willing to look for and appreciate the best in each other.

Spotting Strengths Play Sheet

1. **Set the intention.** Before you head into your next meeting or conversation at work, remind yourself to look for the best in people. You might want to mark a reminder in your diary next to the appointment time, or use an alarm on your smartphone to cue your strength-spotting habit.

2. **Look at what you're seeing.** As things get underway, choose a particular person to really focus on. Look for the moments where this person is more engaged, energized, and enjoying what they're talking about or doing. Often their bodies will literally start to lean in to the conversation, their body language might become more animated, and their tone of voice and pace of speech tend to be uplifted. Make a brief note of what they are talking about or doing in these moments.

3. **Match the strengths.** As you leave the meeting or conversation, use the table of character strengths below to help you spot which strengths the person you were focused on may have been using in these moments. This won't always be obvious, so record your hunches and use the virtue categories to guide what you captured in your snapshot. Were they using their:

    -   **Head strengths:** sharing their latest new ideas or a great piece of research they've just discovered; challenging your mind with new possibilities; or urging you to look at the bigger picture and different perspectives.

    -   **Heart Strengths:** willing to take risks; persevering no matter how difficult things were getting; telling it like it is; or full of energy and vitality around what they're doing.

    -   **Strength of Others:** taking the time to really listen and understand what others need; proposing or performing acts of kindness; or helping to understand people's emotions and motivations.

Spotting Strengths Play Sheet (continued)

- **Strength of Self:** regulating their choices, emotions, and behaviors; demonstrating forgiveness and mercy; delivering the plan no matter what challenges they encounter; or happiest out of the spotlight where they can get on with what needs to be done.

- **Strengths of Community:** making sure things are fair; organizing others to make things happen; or willingly supporting the team to make the whole stronger than the parts.

- **Strengths of Spirit:** inspiring others with a sense of meaning; giving people hope; making people laugh; appreciating others; and connecting you to the true, good and possible in the physical, mental and spiritual world around you.

4. **Look again:** Before you head into your next encounter with the person you observed, look at what you noticed last time and see if the same strengths, or different ones, appear. Continue this process until you feel confident that you understand what this person looks like at their best.

As you begin to spot their strengths, experiment with different ways you might ask this person to help you with specific tasks that are geared towards the strengths you're seeing. Think about how you can communicate and connect with them around their strengths to have more impact. Notice if there are areas where your strengths may be colliding.

And, most importantly, give them strengths-based appreciation and feedback. Acknowledge the strengths they're developing and tell them why you value and appreciate these at work. For example, if you think they have the strength of curiosity, you might say something like, "Thanks for taking the time to meet today; I really valued the questions you were asking to help us get a better outcome on this project."

The Six Virtue Clusters of Character Strengths

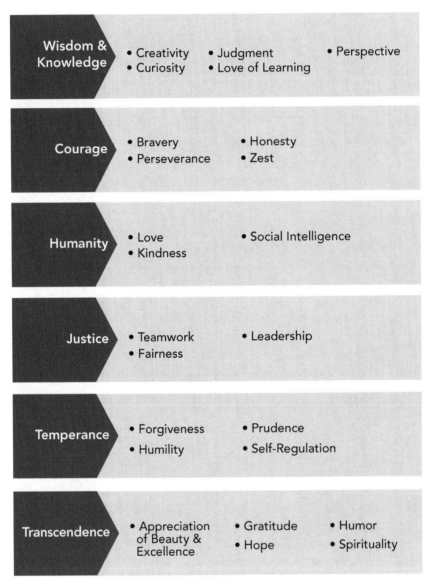

Wisdom & Knowledge
- Creativity
- Curiosity
- Judgment
- Love of Learning
- Perspective

Courage
- Bravery
- Perseverance
- Honesty
- Zest

Humanity
- Love
- Kindness
- Social Intelligence

Justice
- Teamwork
- Fairness
- Leadership

Temperance
- Forgiveness
- Humility
- Prudence
- Self-Regulation

Transcendence
- Appreciation of Beauty & Excellence
- Gratitude
- Hope
- Humor
- Spirituality

Becoming a Strengths-Led Organization

Organizations are increasingly coming to understand that their people are the most valuable asset they have. As the war for good talent continues, our awareness that it costs between seventy and two hundred percent of a person's salary to replace them means that being able to recruit, develop, and reward strengths is good business sense.[8] Of course, knowing is one thing and doing is quite another, so how can your organization put these ideas into practice?

There is a delicate balance to be struck as you look for ways to develop strengths across your organization's people-management systems and practices. When it comes to unleashing peak performance in teams, it's important to maintain a diversity of strengths and opportunities for growth. While it's tempting to use tools like the VIA Survey for recruitment, there is also a real danger of reading too much into these results, "boxing" people in, and overlooking the unique ways each person is motivated to develop their strengths.

To strike this balance, rather than relying too heavily on assessment tools designed to identify, but not necessarily to change behavior, we recommend complementing these tools with the strengths-based change framework known as *Appreciative Inquiry*. Created to find and build on the true, the good, and the possible, this approach has been used to unleash the potential in people, organizations, and even entire cities or countries.[9] In fact, Part B of this book, which helps you develop your own strengths, uses the Appreciative Inquiry framework.

Devised by Professor David Cooperrider at Case Western University, there are five principles that guide this framework[10] and offer important insights about human behavior that are often overlooked in organizations. These insights are worth embedding at the heart of your people-management processes.

1. **Poetic Principle**—what you focus on grows. When you ask people and their managers to identify the flaws in their performance, have you noticed you never reach the bottom of the list? There's always one more thing to fix. If you ask people and their managers to identify the strengths

in their performance, the same thing occurs. What could you achieve if you really understood the people assets you had to build upon?

2. **Simultaneity Principle**—every action we take is preceded by a question, yet we're so busy telling people what we want them to do that we never think to ask. Change begins with the first question you pose, so what are you asking people about when, where, and how they perform at their best at work?

3. **Anticipatory Principle**—positive images pull us forward. We saw the evidence for this in Chapter 4, but how vivid are the feelings, sounds, and images that you encourage your people to create when it comes to their future in your organization? Have you instilled enough hope so they believe that tomorrow will be better than today and that they can make it so?

4. Positive Principles—positive emotions lead to positive actions. How do your people-management systems and practices leave people feeling? Do they dread them? Or do they look forward to setting their annual goals, getting feedback, and hearing their performance reviews? Do they walk away from this process excited and energized about what they can achieve next?

5. **Constructionist Principle**—our words create worlds. The stories we help people to create about their performance—"good" or "bad," "capable" or "inept," "people person" or "task focused"—determine the way they feel and act at work. Think about the phenomenon of growth mindsets, which we looked at in Chapter 4. Do your people-development practices help people focus on stories that build the confidence, optimism, and effort required for success?[11]

If you're reading this list and shaking your head because your people-management practices appear to be doing the opposite of these principles, don't feel too bad. Traditionally, most organizations have viewed their people as machines to be fixed and controlled, rather than as living systems of infinite strengths to be unleashed. Fortunately, Cooperrider also found that there is a very simple framework to embed these principles in the way you can positively change behavior.

Known as the 4-D Framework (**Discover, Dream, Design, Deliver**) it begins by focusing on an appreciative question or topic of inquiry that you want to see more of from your people. What do you want to grow? What do you want to see improve? For example, this book's focus is: "How can you unleash your potential at work by developing your strengths?"

The 4-D Framework is as follows:

- **"Discover" the best of the past:** What are the best examples of when your chosen topic of inquiry was working well? For example, in Chapter 3 we asked you to reflect on the high-point moments—those times that were memorable and stood out at work and helped you identify the strengths you'd been using.

- **"Dream" of what's possible:** What would the future look like if you consistently had the best examples happening at work? For example, in Chapter 4 we invited you to imagine a strengths-fueled future at work.

- **"Design" what might be:** What are the pathways that'll take you from where you are now to the future you're dreaming about? For example, in Chapter 5 we suggested that you create a hope map and explore the pathways to move you toward your "want to" goal.

- **"Deliver" what will be:** What changes are you actually willing to make? For example, in Chapter 6 we helped you commit to taking the first step (in this case, your daily strengths-development habit) to act on your chosen pathways.[12]

It sounds simple enough, but how can you apply this strengths-based change framework within your existing people-management processes and systems?

Recruiting for Strengths

The most effective place to start is ensuring you're finding the right match between people's strengths and the jobs you're offering during the recruitment process. Get this right, and it can save you a lot of wasted time, effort, and money—with a bad hiring decision currently estimated to cost approximately thirty percent of someone's first-year earnings.[13] In fact, Tony Hsieh—the CEO of online retailing giant Zappos—once estimated that his own bad hires had cost him well over $100 million.[14]

167

You can use Appreciative Inquiry—with or without people's VIA strength survey results or other assessment tools—to guide the way you recruit people by focusing on an appreciative topic of inquiry like: "At their best, what is this person capable of achieving?" Just setting this goal for the interview will help counter your (as the interviewer) hard-wired negativity bias that causes you to focus too heavily on finding weaknesses in candidates. After all, you're not trying to hire the person with the fewest weaknesses; you're trying to hire the person with the most strengths.

Some interviewers will fear that this may mean flaws are overlooked, but our brains are already so well trained to spot potential problems. Based on Michelle's experience, we believe that a good interviewer will quickly spot the gaps and potential weaknesses in what the interviewee shares (or doesn't share) when answering these questions. When using Appreciative Inquiry, there is also no reason to avoid asking about areas of concern. Our advice, however, is to spend most of the interview process helping the candidate to feel safe and positive so you can really interrogate their strengths, and only induce anxiety or fear (natural responses when we feel our shortcomings are being probed) if you have ongoing concerns about how they will perform under stress.

With this in mind, we recommend the following guidelines for job application forms and interviews:

- Identify the candidate's current capabilities, based on their past performance.

- Assess the candidate's potential, based on their aspirations for the future.

- Determine the level of development required to bring out the candidate's best.

- Find candidates who are willing to learn, grow, and be accountable.

- Ensure candidates are a good match for the job opportunity, the team, and your organizational culture.

For example, a job interview using the Appreciative Inquiry framework may unfold as follows:

- **Discover:** "Tell me about a time you felt the most alive, engaged, and proud of your work? What was happening? What were you doing? What circumstances allowed for such an incredible experience? What made it so memorable for you?"

  Stories about past performance are easily elicited by using the phrase, "Tell me about . . .". You'll uncover stories of strengths in action by using words like, "most", "best", or "proudest". If you wish, you can prompt for specific examples of character strengths from their VIA Survey results by adding questions like, "Which strengths were you drawing on?"

  Reflecting on their best past experiences allows a candidate to build a sense of confidence, which sparks positive emotions that flood the brain with dopamine and serotonin. This enables them to think quickly, creatively, laterally, and collaboratively during the interview process.[15] It allows you to see them performing at their best, as well as to hear about their examples of peak performance, so you can determine if they will meet your job requirements.

- **Dream:** "Imagine you're successful in securing the role and three years from now we're sitting down to conduct your performance review. What would you have achieved? Why would your clients rave about working with you? What do your colleagues say when they describe your work?"

  Try prompting for responses that elicit the sounds (what will people be saying), feelings (what will you be proudest of), and actions (what will you be doing) they most want to experience at work. Again, you can explore what their strengths-fueled future will look like by adding questions like, "Which of your character strengths will you be consistently using?"

  Inviting someone during the interview process to share their hopes for the future ensures that their positive emotions continue to flow. It also allows you to see their motivations—the things that are internally and externally driving them—unmasked. The positive images they share are like a crystal ball into the future, offering an insight into the actions they'll be most invested in pursuing. This is the truth of what they most want for their lives. You need to consider carefully how it matches the opportunities and aspirations of your organization.

- **Design:** "If you had three hopes for your development, coaching, and on-the-job experiences to help you move from where you are today to the future you've just described, what would they be?"

Your intention here is to prompt them to explore pathways forward. This is a great place to challenge weaknesses by presenting different obstacles they may face—asking how they'd overcome them, and how they'd maintain their motivation, willpower, and grit to reach their long-term goals. Again, you can explore how they'd use their strengths to move forward by asking questions like, "Which of your character strengths do you think will be the most important to develop in order to make these hopes a reality? What support will you need in order to ensure that you're not underplaying or overplaying specific strengths?"

Asking the candidate to detail the pathways that will move them from where they are today to achieving the dream they've described for you helps to illuminate the development, coaching, and on-the-job experiences they're likely to need in order to reach their potential. Remember, you get a better return on investment by building on their strengths, so listen carefully to how they want to improve themselves. Be aware of what they're not identifying, and if this is of concern, probe further to see if these are possible weaknesses you need to take into account.

- **Deliver:** "Based on this interview process, and regardless of the final result, if there was one thing you'd start doing differently tomorrow to unleash more of your potential at work, what would it be?"

Get them to focus on the action they are willing to be accountable for taking. Keep this question general. Don't lead them. Michelle calls this the "skin-in-the-game test" because you can tell by someone's answers how committed they are to realizing their own potential. If you want to explore specific strengths you can ask, "What will you do to develop your character strengths more following this conversation?"

Testing the candidate's willingness to take accountability for their own development allows you to gauge their growth mindsets. Their answers will provide insight into their ability to take control of their future, or their likelihood to become a victim of your organization's processes and policies. It also allows you to explore their resourcefulness, networks of support, and their ability to solve problems creatively.

You can find a detailed strengths-based interview guide at <u>michellemcquaid.com/strengths</u> if you'd like more recruitment ideas.

Investing in the Development of Strengths

Once you're hiring for strengths, it makes sense to invest your organization's development efforts into cultivating the potential you've recruited. With organizations around the world spending over 130 billion dollars annually on addressing perceived skills gaps in their people,[16] it pays to ensure your budget for formal training programs, on-the-job learning opportunities, and one-on-one coaching, delivers the most effective return on your investment.

You can help your managers or human resource teams create strengths-based development templates, or have conversations with your employees by focusing on an appreciative topic of inquiry such as, "How can we develop your potential to consistently perform at your best at work?" To guide people's reflections, we recommend asking them to complete or update their VIA Survey results at the start of this process. Alternatively, you can choose to interpret the word "strengths" in the examples that follow in a much broader sense.

The Appreciative Inquiry framework can be applied to development conversations as follows:

- **Discover:** "Tell me about the best experiences you've had to develop your strengths at work." If you want to dig deeper into how different types of development support their growth, you might also ask, "What were the best on-the-job experiences that developed your strengths? Who are the people you've learned from the most when it comes to developing your strengths? What's been the best training program or other formal learning experience where you really felt your strengths lift to new levels?"

- **Dream:** "If you could have more opportunities to develop your strengths, what do you think you could achieve? What would you feel most excited about tackling at work? What differences would your colleagues notice about how you performed your work? What would your clients say about these changes?" You may want to anchor it to a specific time period. For example, "What could you achieve in the year ahead?" Or, you can leave it open-ended depending on the priorities of your organization.

- **Design:** "If you had three opportunities that were within your control to develop your strengths further, what would they be?" Again, you may want to dig a little deeper into this question and specifically ask, "What kind of on-the-job opportunities, coaching, or formal training do you need?" This will help you to get a clear picture on what the person's development plan is likely to require.

- **Deliver:** "If there was one strength you'd focus on developing immediately, where would you start?" This will give you an insight into what they're willing to commit to and be accountable for when it comes to their own development, rather than just expecting that you or the organization will do it all for them.

You can find a detailed strengths-based development guide at michellemcquaid.com/strengths if you'd like more examples.

Providing Strengths Feedback

Now that you've created expectations for your employees that their strengths are valued, it's important that you follow through and provide strengths-based feedback on their performance. With eighty-one percent of employees reporting that they're motivated to work harder when their boss shows appreciation for their work,[17] this one simple process could save your organization billions of dollars in lost productivity. When managers give their employees strengths-based feedback, it helps people understand why they're valued, how they can develop these strengths further, and it improves their self-belief, confidence, and resilience for new challenges.

Providing strengths-based feedback doesn't mean you only discuss what's going right. After all, just because a strength leads to success in one situation doesn't mean it will work in every context. Managers need to be taught how to provide feedback that helps employees to determine which strengths are most appropriate for specific contexts. For example, dialing down their *curiosity* and dialing up their *perseverance* against a tight deadline.

To guide managers on giving strengths-based feedback, rather than just using the Appreciative Inquiry framework to create questions, you can use it to prompt them for the kind of observations they want to share. For example, the focus of inquiry for this conversation might be, "What do we really value about your efforts and results at work?" If the manager has access to the employees' VIA Survey results, then it helps to align feedback to these results. If not, then the strengths-spotting techniques outlined in the previous play sheet (page 162) can also help them prepare for this conversation.

The Appreciative Inquiry framework can be applied to strengths-feedback conversations as follows:

- **Discover:** "I've really noticed and valued your engagement, energy, and enjoyment in your work when . . ." Then the manager could share their observations about when they have seen the employees' strengths being used well.

- **Dream:** "If you had more moments like this in the year ahead, I believe you could . . ." Then the manager could share their insights into the potential they see in the employee and ways his/her strengths could be built upon to deliver outstanding results.

- **Design:** "To achieve this, I'd like to see you developing your strengths more by . . ." Then the manager could detail the strengths and pathways they'd like this employee prioritize to perform even more effectively.

- **Deliver:** "I'd really appreciate it if you could try to use your strengths over the next few days to . . ." Then the manager could offer a small, immediate change the employee can make to improve his/her performance and the team's results.

You can find a detailed strengths-based feedback guide at <u>michellemcquaid.</u>

<u>com/strengths</u> for your managers.

These questions and statements are intended only as examples. Be sure you give managers the permission to phrase suggested Appreciative Inquiry approaches in words that feel authentic to how they naturally engage with their employees. Based on Michelle's experience, we believe that the hardest part of helping managers to feel confident about this approach is helping them to flip their mindset to find the best rather than the worst in your people. As Jack Welch once said, "When you were made a leader you weren't given a crown, you were given the responsibility to bring out the best in others."

We hope that throughout your journey from Parts A to C of this book, you've learned: *what* strengths are; *why* they are so valuable in the context of your work; and *how* to discover your own strengths, dream of a strengths-fuelled future, design pathways forward, deliver on your strengths consistently, and embed your strengths in your work. We wish you well as you take this strengths blueprint and apply it in your world to bring you more engagement, energy, and happiness at work.

APPENDIX

APPRECIATION OF BEAUTY AND EXCELLENCE

Looks Like . . .

is your capacity to notice and enjoy the beautiful and/or excellent things you find in the world around you. You appreciate a wide variety of things, such as the physical environment, a demonstration of someone's abilities or virtues, or even an interesting piece of knowledge. [1]

At Your Best . . .

You're at your best when your workplace values excellence, where you and those around you can openly express admiration,[2] and where you're exposed to a variety of beautiful and excellent experiences. For example, you like it when the exceptional work of your colleagues is recognized and displayed.

Challenged By . . .

Because you thrive on noticing the good, you find it challenging to work in environments where the people around you prefer a critical or negative attitude.[3] For example, you might feel frustrated when people pick out what you've done wrong on a project and don't also acknowledge what you've done exceptionally well.

Shadow Side . . .

The shadow side of appreciation is perfectionism, where only the best is accepted. Imagine, for example, someone who can't work at their desk unless everything is in its proper place or hesitates to share their work because it's not yet "good enough". To avoid this shadow side, it is important to appreciate the good without being intolerant to the less-than-perfect.

Develop By . . .

- **Creating a workspace you love:**

  This might include a nice set of stationary, photos of loved ones or favorite places, a comfortable chair, or a decorative plant. Make your work area a place of sanctuary.

- **Making time to reconnect with nature:**

  Once a day take a few minutes and head outside. Sit under a tree, or walk through a park or along a river. Things that are green or blue are great for your wellbeing.

- **Hunting for greatness:**

  Look for the uplifting moments of excellence in your day that inspire you to be better. You might observe a great example of teamwork between colleagues, or notice someone who is making great progress on a challenging task.

- **Keeping an inspiration file:**

  Keep a folder to record the various sources of excellence you come across, and use it to inspire you when you feel like you need a boost. Your file might include photos, articles, and your own notes.

BRAVERY

Looks Like . . .

Bravery describes your willingness to rise up and confront difficult or threatening situations.[1] You take the time to acknowledge and evaluate the risks involved in facing up to a challenge, and endeavor to derive the best outcome from tough conditions[2] while remaining in charge of any feelings of fear that you experience.[3]

At Your Best . . .

Beyond your ability to demonstrate courage in the face of a physical threat, you can use your strength of bravery at work to confront psychological and moral challenges.[4] For example, your bravery may enable you to persevere through a tough deadline, own up to a mistake you've made, or stick up for a colleague who's not being supported by their team members.

Challenged By . . .

Because you like to face up to challenges, you struggle in circumstances where you're not given the freedom to stand up and take action in a courageous way.[5] For example, this might occur if you're deterred from standing up for a colleague because you're under the impression that you'll be fired for it.

Shadow Side . . .

When overplayed, your bravery can turn into recklessness.[6] This means that you will take unnecessary risks in circumstances where the safer option is more sensible. To dial down this shadow side, always weigh-up the situation to determine whether it's more beneficial to push for the risky option, or stick to the more cautious and steady pathway. Rather than diving in feet-first every time, it's often wise to pilot novel ideas to minimize any associated risks.

Develop By . . .

- **Stretching outside your comfort zone:**

  Try to start each day by stepping outside of your comfort zone, whether it's in a big or small way. Endeavor to take action on one thing that you would normally put off for a later time.

- **Cultivating unexpected partnerships:**

  Each week, make time to meet with someone you wouldn't normally interact with but whom you think will have a positive impact on your day-to-day work.[7]

- **Finding your heroes:**

  Each day, take notice of one person at work who is courageously showing up or stepping forward in a way that is unexpected. This will help you to reinforce the narrative that courageous behavior is respected, making you more likely to be brave yourself when necessary.

CREATIVITY

Looks Like . . .

Creativity describes your preference for producing new ideas and executing behaviors that are original. You're good at generating novelty, and are able to apply this strength in ways that are useful and beneficial to yourself and others.[1]

At Your Best . . .

You're at your best when working in a flexible environment,[2] where you're given the room and the support to think outside the box and be innovative in order to solve problems and make things work. You thrive on novelty.

Challenged By . . .

Because you prefer to explore new ways of doing things, you can be challenged when working in heavily constricted environments, such as those that run on strict deadlines or rely upon procedures that are set in stone.[3]

Shadow Side . . .

The shadow side of creativity emerges when you become more interested in creating than delivering. This can cause you to become so enamored with your ideas that you lose sight of the commercial value of what your organization requires. It can also result in you constantly tinkering with ideas so they're never quite finished, or becoming bored with an idea once it moves into delivery. To overcome this shadow side, try to concentrate on channeling your creativity into ideas and innovations that will deliver the goals and requirements of the organization.

Develop By . . .

- **Making time for creative exploration:**

  Keep creative tools such as marker pens and a sketchpad readily at hand. Spend at least ten minutes each day using these tools to explore a project you're currently working on by drawing or mind-mapping ideas and approaches. You can do this yourself when you arrive at work or with your team during meetings.

- **Finding seven solutions:**

  Push your brain to think more creatively by coming up with at least seven different solutions to problems you may be trying to solve at work. Most of us stop at one or two, but the unexpected and unimagined possibilities usually emerge when we're pushed to go beyond the obvious.

- **Play with your creativity:**

  Download an app on your smartphone or tablet that promotes more creative and free thinking. Allow yourself ten minutes each day to explore your creativity through this outlet.

CURIOSITY

Looks Like . . .

Curiosity refers to your appetite for knowledge. You constantly want to learn more by delving into the information you come across and engaging in new experiences. When you observe an opportunity to learn or participate in something new, you take action in order to feed your desire to keep growing.[1]

At Your Best . . .

You thrive when you're able to put the new knowledge or practices that you have acquired to work in order to solve challenging problems or meet particular goals.[2] You love to explore the best practices to adopt, test new approaches, research market opportunities, understand customer drivers, and figure out ways to get a handle on your competitors.

Challenged By . . .

You love having the permission to explore dynamically, and as a result, you find it particularly challenging to work in situations where your performance is heavily monitored or measured,[3] or you're given strict boundaries to adhere to. Under such circumstances, your intrinsic motivation to explore is depleted as you become more focused on the task at hand rather than the freedom to learn.

Shadow Side . . .

Curiosity can be problematic when it leads to becoming too fascinated with exploring ideas without taking any action. This leaves you paralyzed in the search, where the learning you undertake is wasted in terms of the value of application. It is important to make an effort to translate your curiosity from knowledge to practice in order to help generate real-world outcomes.

Develop By . . .

- **Learning one new thing each day:**

  Make a note of something you learned through conversing with a colleague, reading an article, or listening during a meeting. In your note, include a brief explanation of why what you learned matters, as well as how this knowledge can be applied.

- **Thinking in questions:**

  Every action we take is preceded by a question. See if you can find the questions that need to be asked to create the outcomes you want. For example, create agenda questions for your meetings rather than agenda items.

- **Looking for alternative explanations:**

  Avoid jumping to conclusions by challenging your beliefs and assumptions. Ask yourself, "Is this the only explanation for what's unfolding?", and note how these different stories make you want to feel and act.

FAIRNESS

Looks Like . . .

Fairness refers to your strong sense of what you believe to be right, and your desire to act in accordance with these beliefs. You care deeply about others and are good at understanding other people's perspectives.[1]

At Your Best . . .

You're at your best in environments where the people around you support your need to act in congruence with your beliefs about right and wrong, and where your desire to act fairly is shared by your colleagues.[2] For example, in such an environment, you would expect to have the autonomy to freely speak up when you believe something is wrong.

Challenged By . . .

You particularly struggle to work in environments where your beliefs are not supported.[3] For example, your desire to do what you think is right will be undermined in circumstances where you feel your work is having a negative impact on an individual or group of people.

Shadow Side . . .

If overplayed, fairness can lead you to become detached from your work.[4] That is, if you feel your workplace or team are not behaving equitably, you may try to protect yourself by detaching from the choices and actions that happen both around and within you. You may at times also find yourself getting too worked up or upset when you believe something is unfair. To manage this shadow side, consider whether what you're fighting for is worth holding onto in the given context, or whether it might be more appropriate to let go.

Develop By . . .

- **Being fair to others:**

  Each week, invest in one action that you believe will make your workplace a little bit fairer for one of your colleagues. You might, for example, acknowledge when someone has been unfairly treated and talk to them about it, or even offer some positive feedback to someone who deserves it.

- **Owning your mistakes:**

  When you make mistakes, don't be afraid to take ownership and admit to yourself that you've done wrong.[5]

- **Being willing to forgive:**

  Monitor the internal conversation you have with yourself when you or someone around you makes a mistake. Give yourself the space to recognize that we are all allowed to get things wrong sometimes, and that equally we can be forgiven. Be willing to forgive yourself, as you would be willing to forgive others.

FORGIVENESS

Looks Like . . .

Forgiveness describes your preference for moving on after a transgression and your desire to mend fences with the person who has done you wrong.[1] When you show forgiveness, your motivation to respond negatively following an incident of wrongdoing transforms into the desire to cultivate and preserve a harmonious relationship with the transgressor.[2]

At Your Best . . .

You excel in environments where the people around you seek your forgiveness when they've done you wrong,[3] because you prefer to preserve your relationships following a transgression. Your ability to avoid excessive negative responses to conflict by forgiving your colleagues enables you to maintain a peaceful workspace when mistakes are made.

Challenged By . . .

Though you're good at mending fences when others have done you wrong, you falter in situations where the people you work with continually commit the same mistakes.[4] This impedes your ability to move forward in the same way that you'd normally be able to. For example, a colleague who repeatedly forgets to check their e-mails or who regularly runs late to meetings, and, consequently, always misses important information, would test you.

Shadow Side . . .

When overplayed, your strength of forgiveness can lead you to become permissive.[5] This means that you can be inclined to allow anyone, including yourself, to get away with anything. You can let people walk all over you, and you may find it difficult to hold yourself accountable for your own actions. To avoid this shadow side, it's important to consider what you respect and what you don't. Know where your boundaries are and be willing to recognize and communicate when they've been crossed.

Develop By . . .

- **Practicing empathy:**

  When you're feeling annoyed or frustrated at someone, build a bridge of empathy that allows you to understand and respect where they might be coming from6 even if you don't entirely agree with their perspective.

- **Showing yourself a little mercy:**

  Each week, try to find one thing to forgive yourself for. It might be for a mistake you made at work, for not being able to deliver on something you promised, or for saying something without fully appreciating the consequences. Instead of beating yourself up, offer yourself the mercy that you would willingly give to others.

- **Disempowering shame:**

  When you notice that a colleague is feeling a sense of shame about their work, help them to unwind this negativity. Reach out and ask them how they're feeling, and create a safe space where they can talk about what's happening. Try to normalize their shameful behavior by helping them to bring it back to earth and put it into perspective.

GRATITUDE

Looks Like . . .

Gratitude is your capacity to experience gratefulness for the good things in your life. You're able to take a moment to notice and appreciate the things that happen to you, or are given to you, which positively influence your life. Furthermore, you're aware that these things are made possible by something or someone beyond yourself, and so it's to this source that you readily express your thanks.[1]

At Your Best . . .

You're able to thrive in environments where there are regular chances to express gratitude.[2] You appreciate being thanked by others, and relish the opportunity to offer your own expressions of gratefulness to your colleagues. By noticing and appreciating the good things in your life, you're able to experience more positive emotions, and less negative emotions like jealousy and resentment.[3]

Challenged By . . .

Because you prefer to be thankful for the good things in life, you struggle to work in environments where people focus more on their rights.[4] You feel frustrated when people take good things for granted, rather than recognizing that someone has gone to the effort to do something helpful or kind for them.

Shadow Side . . .

When gratitude is used as a means of winning someone's favor or persuading someone to do something you want, it becomes ingratiation[5] and is therefore not true gratitude. This shadow side can be avoided by only offering someone your gratitude if it genuinely reflects how you feel, rather than as a means to get something in return.

Develop By . . .

- **Celebrating what's working well:**

  Begin meetings at work by discussing what's been going well recently and expressing appreciation for the efforts people are making.

- **Creating a daily gratitude habit:**

  Genuinely thank one person each day before you leave work for making your day a little better or easier. Be specific in identifying what you're thanking them for, what strengths they were using, and how it positively impacted you.

- **Keeping a gratitude checklist:**

  Throughout your workday, note down all the things that unfold which you are grateful for. Try to find at least three to five things each day. This will be especially helpful on those days when things don't seem to be going the way you'd like.

HONESTY

Looks Like . . .

Your **honesty** describes your ability to be authentic when presenting to both yourself and others, leading you to act and speak in ways that reflect what you really think and feel. You know what your values are and you live by them, preferring not to compromise who you are and what you believe in for the sake of popularity.[1]

At Your Best . . .

You're at your best when you're involved in a task or an activity that aligns with your values and strengths.[2] Under such circumstances, you feel you can act in an authentic way—you're confident that by being yourself you'll get the job done well and without compromising what you believe in.

Challenged By . . .

Because you value authenticity, you struggle to work under circumstances where you're obliged to be deceitful[3] or be unfaithful to your idea of what's right. For example, you might feel very uncomfortable working in a team that tries to boost sales by not being entirely open with its clients.

Shadow Side . . .

The shadow side of honesty can emerge in the form of over-righteousness.[4] This is problematic in that it may leave you feeling like you're above the people around you and can render you blind to the shades of gray that exist between honesty and dishonesty. It's important to understand that different people will value directness in different ways, and that sometimes being blunt is not the best course of action. When you think someone is being dishonest, take the time to ask them what's happening—avoid leaping to conclusions and making assumptions about their intentions.

Develop By . . .

- **Saying it like it is:**

  Each morning, give one person constructive and authentic feedback. It could be about their performance on a current project, or an idea they've recently shared. Be sure that you leave them feeling respected, valued, and appreciated.

- **Walking your talk:**

  Show up at work in the same way that you'd expect the people around you to. Be a living example of the kinds of behaviors you want to see from others.

- **Delivering on your promises:**

  Only make commitments that you can keep, and ensure you're timely in your responses to others. If circumstances change in a way that affects your ability to fulfill your end of a promise, go back and reset the expectations by having an open and transparent conversation about what you can deliver and when.

HOPE

Looks Like . . .

Hope is your capacity to devote consideration to what lies beyond the "here and now". You have goals for the future, you believe they'll be achieved, and you behave in such a way that promotes the realization of this belief.[1] Closely related to optimism, you typically see the glass as half full, enabling you to envision positive outcomes and change plans whenever setbacks get in the way.[2]

At Your Best . . .

Your hope enables you to form visions for your future that are desirable but not irrational. It's a realistic form of optimism that allows you to create clear, plausible, and flexible plans to help you achieve these goals. Guided by this planning, you're able to take action to attain your goals—adapting to any challenges that arise, and maintaining the energy needed to get the job done.[3]

Challenged By . . .

Because you have an optimistic outlook, you can be thwarted when working with people who tend to be pessimistic.[4] These people can drain your willpower and interfere with your ability to plan for a positive future.

Shadow Side . . .

Hope can turn into "false hope" or "Pollyannaism", where your expectations become unrealistic.[5] You might ignore genuine limitations to attaining your goals, or chase goals that are too large. If exercised in its ideal form, hope itself is the remedy to false hope.[6] For example, you would use this strength to establish a rational goal that takes constraints into account, and formulate a plausible plan around these constraints.

Develop By . . .

- **Having a passion project:**

  Even if it's not directly related to your job, spend at least ten minutes each day working on a "want to" project that you're passionate about.[7]

- **Spending time with hopeful colleagues:**

  Hope is contagious, so prioritize your time with hopeful colleagues and notice how they're overcoming the challenges they encounter.[8]

- **Building a hope map:**

  Take a sheet of paper, and on the upper right-hand side, write down a "want to" goal you're trying to achieve. On the upper left-hand side, identify at least three pathways that will move you toward this goal. In the middle, write down the obstacles you may encounter for each pathway. Around the edges of the page, write down what you can do to maintain your willpower and motivation.[9]

HUMILITY

Looks Like . . .

Humility refers to your ability to accurately perceive and evaluate yourself, including your strengths, achievements, weaknesses, and mistakes. You locate this concept of yourself within the bigger picture of the world,[1] and present yourself to others in accordance with who you genuinely are.[2] You're good at seeing the worth in all good things, even if they lie outside of you.[3]

At Your Best . . .

You're at your best when working in an environment where you aren't compelled to regularly advocate your performance and achievements.[4] While you recognize your strengths and successes, you prefer not to publicize these; instead, you'd rather go about your work authentically and let this speak for itself.

Challenged By . . .

Because you're good at keeping your strengths and weaknesses in perspective, you struggle to work with people who feel the need to regularly brag about their achievements. For example, you don't like working in roles where people keep score or are publically ranked on their performance.

Shadow Side . . .

In its excessive form, humility can lead you to engage in self-deprecation.[5] You can speak and think disparagingly about yourself, and may often use humor to put yourself down. To overcome this shadow side, make an active effort to focus on your strengths and understand what you respect and value about yourself. Think about yourself through the lens of your team by asking, "What do I have to offer them?" Recognize that you're not beating your own drum by stepping outside of your comfort zone in this way. Rather, you're helping your team get the most value out of your strengths.

Develop By . . .

- **Owning your stuff:**

  When you've done wrong, be willing to hold yourself accountable and apologize readily.6 Always be willing to learn something from the experience.

- **Letting others shine:**

  When having discussions with people, ask them questions to allow them the opportunity to have the floor and present themselves in the best possible light.

- **Celebrating success:**

  Create a daily habit of celebrating success with at least one other person by recognizing the efforts and accomplishments of yourself and others. Use the language of "we" and "us" rather than "me" and "I" so the celebration feels authentic.

HUMOR

Looks Like . . .

Humor describes your ability to generate and appreciate the lighter side of the moment, whether confronted with a more difficult circumstance or a regular day-to-day situation. You like to experience laughter yourself, and you enjoy and are good at igniting laughter in those around you.[1]

At Your Best . . .

You excel when you're able to use your humor to encourage your colleagues and bring them cheer, especially during excessively stressful times.[2] When facing hardships, your humor can work to your advantage by enabling you to remain in a positive mood[3] rather than becoming overwhelmed by negativity.

Challenged By . . .

Because you often prefer to appreciate the lighter side of life, you find it challenging to work in environments that value seriousness at all times[4] or prefer to dwell only on the heavy side of situations.

Shadow Side . . .

Sometimes humor can be used as a means of deflection. Whether it is used to shield against criticism or to avoid having a difficult conversation, deflection prevents others from really understanding what you're truly experiencing inside.

Develop By . . .

- **Starting your day laughing:**

  As you start work, watch a funny video, read a favorite cartoon, or talk to someone who always makes you smile.

- **Prioritizing play:**

  Play helps you to connect with others, explore ideas, and create new possibilities. Start meetings with a funny quiz, create a games area in the office, or just explore an idea with no intentional outcome.

- **Giving yourself permission to have fun at work:**

  Levity is a valuable and positive business practice found to improve engagement, efficiency, and productivity.[5] What can you do to create a little more fun in your culture?

JUDGMENT

Looks Like . . .

Judgment is your capacity to challenge your own personal assumptions and consider alternative explanations before coming to a conclusion. You're able to consider things from different angles and evaluate the various options that are available. As a result, you're very flexible in your beliefs and opinions whenever new evidence presents itself.[1]

At Your Best . . .

You're at your best when working in an environment that offers opportunities for openness,[2] where you're provided with the time and space to explore decisions thoroughly through examining different options and available evidence.

Challenged By . . .

Because you like to consider things carefully before making final decisions, you struggle in situations where decisions must be made with limited opportunity for prior examination. Furthermore, if you like to "maximize" decisions by always searching for the best choice, you may find yourself constantly wondering whether there's a better option available than the option you chose.[3]

Shadow Side . . .

When you exercise too much judgment, you may render yourself ineffective because you're constantly searching for the perfect answer or overwhelming yourself by asking too many questions. To avoid this shadow side, set decision milestones. Plan where you'd like to be along your decision-making pathway at given times, and use this as a guide to reach conclusions that can be acted upon.

Develop By . . .

- **Seeking out opposites:**

  Once a day, try to find people or sources of information that take diametrically opposing points of view on a topic. Explore and really hear both sides of the argument before deciding how to act.

- **Weighing up your options:**

  Before reaching a final decision, explore the potential outcomes of each option by listing the pros and cons.

- **Playing devil's advocate:**

  Have the courage to ask the tough questions when others are in agreement, especially when you think there could be more to the story than has been explored.[4]

- **Making judgments:**

  Set clear milestones for when decisions have to be made, and communicate the judgment you've reached to someone to avoid procrastination.

KINDNESS

Looks Like . . .

Kindness refers to the readiness and enthusiasm you exhibit toward doing things for other people, whether they're close to you or more distant acquaintances.[1] You're generous to others for their sake, rather than your own. You believe that people are deserving of kindness and don't seek any personal benefit when you invest in others.[2]

At Your Best . . .

You thrive at work when there are plenty of opportunities to do kind things for other people, especially when you know that your actions are having a positive impact on their wellbeing or performance.

Challenged By . . .

Because of your belief that people deserve kind deeds and consideration, you find it difficult to work in an organization that regards the personal needs and wellbeing of its workers to be a low priority.[3]

Shadow Side . . .

The shadow side of kindness emerges when you neglect to show kindness to yourself, which can have a detrimental impact on your own wellbeing and performance. To avoid overplaying your kindness in this way, set limits on whom you give kindness to, as well as what and when you give it. For example, if people are continually asking to "pick your brain for ideas" to the point where you can't get your own work done, try setting aside one time each week for an open coffee date where anyone seeking this kind of support can meet with you and ask their questions. It's also important to realize you're worth helping just as much as others, so don't be afraid to ask for other people's kindness when required.[4]

Develop By . . .

- **Being compassionate:**

  When a colleague is being open about a difficult or challenging experience, try to listen without analyzing or judging what they're telling you. Be there for them and make them feel comfortable and safe.[5]

- **Performing an act of kindness for someone:**

  Do one kind thing for another person each day without being asked or expecting a reward.[6]

- **Speaking kindly to others:**

  Whether it's face to face, over the phone, or through e-mails, use kind words when communicating with other people.[7]

LEADERSHIP

Looks Like . . .

Leadership describes your ability to both organize and encourage others in order to help them accomplish group goals.[1] You help the group to find the best pathways to take, and you're able to maintain team unity and cohesion along the way.[2] You can inspire others to step up, and you connect to each member of the team.[3]

At Your Best . . .

You thrive when you're given the chance to independently manage a team, especially if you're able to play a large role in articulating the group's ambitions and objectives.[4]

Challenged By . . .

You find it especially challenging to work in situations where you're not solely in charge of managing the group, or when you're put in a role that under-utilizes your leadership skills.

Shadow Side . . .

The shadow side of leadership can be observed in circumstances where you rule with an iron fist.[5] In such cases, the wishes and ideas of the people you lead can become manipulated or overruled in favor of your own. Preferring the view from the front seat, you may find it difficult to take on the role of "follower" by allowing others to have the opportunity to be in charge. It's important to remember that leadership is about bringing out the best in others, not just yourself. Try to model the behaviors of a servant leader by being willing to be a follower on some projects in your organization.

Develop By . . .

- **Stepping up:**

    In either a formal or informal capacity, offer to be the leader of a project. Keeping in mind that a leader needs a team, seek out people you would like to invite to join you on the project.

- **Facilitating conversations:**

    When people are finding it difficult to gather their thoughts or develop their ideas during meetings, offer to help guide the discussion. To avoid facing resentment, remember to offer but not force your leadership upon the group.

- **Getting inspired:**

    Each day, savor one great example of leadership that you observe both inside and outside of your organization. Focus on what you'd like to emulate yourself, and take notes that'll help you to channel these leaders through your own work. Your notes might include points such as how the leader carries themselves, how they handle difficult situations, and how they get people on board.

LOVE

Looks Like...

Love is your capacity to foster and value the relationships you have with others.[1] Depending upon the nature of the relationship—whether it be a family member, friend, romantic partner, boss, or colleague—love takes on different forms of expression.[2] You place the highest value on relationships that involve mutuality and closeness, where you feel like you're able to both give and receive love.[3]

At Your Best . . .

When working in environments where there's a range of circumstances in which you can develop and foster strong relationships with others, you will excel.[4] You care about the people that you lead, and you can use your strength of love to foster better relationships with them.

Challenged By . . .

Because you place great value on close relationships, you find it most challenging to be in a workplace where the people around you show little interest in caring for the wellbeing and emotional welfare of themselves and the people around them.[5]

Shadow Side . . .

In its full form, this strength involves both the capacity to give and receive love. However, sometimes you may find yourself giving so much love to others that you leave nothing left for yourself. It is important to negotiate this balance when exercising love, so you can take care of your own needs as much as the needs of those around you.

Develop By . . .

- **Loving others:**

  Perform one act of love each day by checking in with a colleague to show them they are respected, valued, and appreciated. You might thank them for something, make them a cup of coffee, or just have a conversation with them about how they're doing.

- **Loving yourself:**

  Find one thing each day that you can do to care for and nurture yourself. This might include some light exercise, a healthy snack, meditation, or listening to your favorite music.

- **Positively resonating with others:**

  Share an experience of positive emotion with someone, and take the time to invest in the feelings of warmth and trust that naturally arise from this.

LOVE OF LEARNING

Looks Like . . .

Your **love of learning** refers to the willingness you have to acquire knowledge or skills, the joy you experience while doing it, and the confidence you feel in your ability to reach particular learning outcomes. You learn for the sake of learning, enabling you to persevere with your quest to find out more whenever the task proves difficult or you experience failure.[1]

At Your Best . . .

You thrive when you find yourself in situations where you're given the opportunity to utilize a new skill or further develop your knowledge.

Challenged By . . .

Because you relish the chance to grow your knowledge and skills, you struggle to work in an environment where there is limited possibility to learn new things.[2] For example, you may find it challenging to perform roles that involve business-as-usual situations, where strategies, processes and approaches are set in stone and there's limited appetite for improvement.

Shadow Side . . .

A love of learning can negatively manifest itself in the form of a know-it-all demeanor,[3] where you come across as believing you already know all there is to know about everything. This can be intimidating for others to encounter, and as a result can distance you from them. To avoid this shadow side, it's important to be open to new ideas, and allow others to express their knowledge without trying to show them up with what you know.

Develop By . . .

- **Growing your experiences:**

  Sign up and get involved in new experiences that will enable you to learn something tomorrow that you don't know today.

- **Savoring knowledge:**

  Experience the joy of learning for the sake of learning itself. Take the time to learn one new thing each day that is relevant to your work. It could be relevant to the organization you work for, or to the industry in a broader sense.

- **Learning about people:**

  Try to meet one new colleague or client each week. Have a conversation with them about what they do, focusing on which aspects they really enjoy, as well as what they are most challenged by. Attend networking events, such as conferences, to learn from others who work in your field.

PERSEVERANCE

Looks Like . . .

Perseverance describes your ability to keep at the tasks you set yourself. Even though you confront challenges along the way, you make a choice to keep working toward your goals without letting these discouragements or barriers impede you.[1] Not only are you good at getting things done, you also take pleasure in the accomplishment of your goals.[2]

At Your Best . . .

You flourish when you're confronted with a task that entails that you stay engaged and work hard.[3] It might be that you're given a long-term project to work on that requires an enduring commitment, or perhaps you have to push through several challenges and mishaps in order to execute a project.

Challenged By . . .

Because you make a concerted effort to get the job done—even in the face of hardships and mishaps—you feel that your efforts are devalued when your competence is not recognized.[4] You feel particularly frustrated when people ignore your hard work or fail to acknowledge the difficulties you had to push through to finish a project or task.

Shadow Side . . .

Your perseverance becomes overplayed when it leads you to pursue goals and tasks obsessively.[5] Such obsession leaves you feeling like you're unable to stop pushing yourself to reach your target, even when you're exhausted and on the brink of burnout. As such, you'll resist putting on the breaks even when it's actually more beneficial to do so, and avoid taking the time to rest and revitalize when necessary. To manage this shadow side, always remember that relentless perseverance works to the detriment of the outcomes you're trying to achieve, and taking a break is beneficial to your goal pursuit.

Develop By . . .

- **Delivering what matters most:**

  Each morning, set yourself a few small goals that you will accomplish before the end of your workday. Consider how you'll manage your time to ensure you prioritize the delivery of these goals.

- **Finding your rhythm:**

  Due to your natural ultradian rhythm, throughout the day you'll experience ninety to one-hundred-minute bursts of alertness. At the end of each cycle, it's important to take a short break in order to maximize your performance and avoid burnout.

- **Setting yourself a clear plan:**

  Determine what you want to achieve over the next six to twelve months, and create a week-by-week plan that will enable you to move from where you are now to where you want to be. Commit to implementing your plan, and monitor your progress as you move from one week to the next.

PERSPECTIVE

Looks Like . . .

Perspective describes your capacity to view situations in a way that resonates meaningfully for both yourself and the people you share your views with. You're good at looking at a situation from different angles, and because of this, others appreciate your insights and will often seek your counsel.[1]

At Your Best . . .

YYou thrive when you're engaged in work projects or tasks that require you to draw on your experience and expertise.[2] You feel like you're at your best when you can use what you know to inform the way you go about your own work, and communicate your insights with your team members to help them fulfill their role on a project.

Challenged By . . .

Your appetite to acquire wisdom leaves you feeling frustrated when there's limited opportunity to learn new things, engage in new experiences, and have personal growth.[3] You feel like you're not getting any wiser when you're performing roles that require you to get things done according to a strict formula or manual. When your role is heavily documented and systematized in this way, you feel there is a lack of opportunity to share your views and offer advice to others.

Shadow Side . . .

Because you have a strong sense of perspective, you may at times look for too many opportunities to impart your wisdom to others and give them advice when it's not welcome. It's important to recognize that while your perspective might be insightful, there is a right time and place to share your views with others. To help you manage this, ask yourself whether your advice will genuinely be of value to those you share it with.

Develop By . . .

- **Learning from others:**

    Take the time each day to read biographies about other business people who inspire you or work in your field. Take note of the key lessons that they present to help guide you on your own career journey.[4]

- **Considering "in what context, for what outcome?":**

    To find the best action to take to achieve the outcome you desire, ask yourself this question before deciding which pathway to choose.

- **Making the complex simple:**

    Look for ways to translate theories to real-world practice. Think of simple ways to explain complex ideas so they make sense to others.

PRUDENCE

Looks Like . . .

Prudence can be defined as your ability to think and act in ways that are conducive to the attainment of your future aspirations and long-term goals. You think about and place value on the future, and like to plan for what lies ahead. You readily consider how your decisions will affect certain outcomes and are good at regulating your behaviors in the present in line with your goals.[1]

At Your Best . . .

You thrive when you're given the space and time to think about what your aspirations are,[2] to devise a plan around these goals, and to take the necessary steps to execute your plan.

Challenged By . . .

Because you like to act in accordance with long-term goals, you can be thwarted when forced to make a spontaneous decision due to the arising of unexpected circumstances.[3] This might occur when you're involved in an ambiguous project, or given a tight deadline to complete an important task.

Shadow Side . . .

Prudence can at times manifest itself as over-cautiousness. This means you can be afraid to take risks or be spontaneous. Your need to adhere to the plan can make you appear like a "stick in the mud," where you close yourself off to new and unexpected opportunities. To help you dial down this strength, always keep in mind that your plan is but one path toward your goal. Try to hold your commitments a little more lightly and give things the chance to evolve naturally, keeping an open mind about what could arise, and not being so rigid that you miss new opportunities.

Develop By . . .

- **Planning ahead:**

  Before taking action, make time to consider and picture the potential outcomes of a choice you have to make. Think of what the consequences might look like within a one-year timeframe, as well as in the longer-term of five to ten years.[4]

- **Sticking to the plan:**

  Whenever you have a goal in mind, set clear milestones that need to be achieved along the way. Create a daily habit to use tools such as project plans, and try new online offerings like asana.com to ensure what you promise is delivered on time and on budget.

- **Thinking before you speak:**

  When you're in a meeting, give yourself the time and space to pause and reflect on what you'll say next.[5] Once you've taken this moment and feel comfortable, offer up your idea. Don't be afraid to ask for extra time for reflection if you feel that it's needed.

- **Making room for spontaneity:**

  To help you remain flexible on the journey toward your goal, create a daily habit to step back from your plan and look at the bigger picture. Are there new opportunities emerging you should seize upon? Are there obstacles on the horizon you need to be ready for? Should you slow down any deliverables to ensure better quality?

SELF-REGULATION

Looks Like . . .

Self-regulation describes your ability to remain in charge of what you think, which feelings you experience, and what actions you engage in. You live in a disciplined way in order to meet the various goals you've set for yourself. Depending on what the situation calls for, you have the ability to overrule your maladaptive impulses, as well as to generate adaptive actions that counter your first inclinations.[1]

At Your Best . . .

Because you thrive on being disciplined, you excel when you're working in an environment with well-defined rules and boundaries[2] that are stringently implemented. For example, you're good at working on projects that have a well-articulated deadline, and engaging with tasks that can't be completed by taking shortcuts.

Challenged By . . .

You can struggle during those times where you're exposed to high levels of stress[3] or when you're physically exhausted. When the workload becomes unbearable, or the hours become too long, this can impede your ability to stay in control of your responses with the same level of discipline you normally exhibit.

Shadow Side . . .

Self-regulation can be overplayed when it causes inhibition.[4] This means you can at times find it difficult to respond spontaneously or act in a way that feels natural to you. To overcome this shadow side, try to consciously play around with some of your routines. By introducing some openness and flexibility to your habits, you'll enable yourself to be in charge of your choices rather than letting your routines control you.

Develop By . . .

- **Starting early:**

  Identify the most important tasks you have to do each day, and do these first thing in the morning when your self-regulation levels are at their highest.

- **Managing your emotions:**

  Throughout your day, try to be mindful of how you're feeling and how this is causing you to act. Identify the things that trigger your worst behaviors, and think of ways you can manage these situations more effectively to get the results you want.

- **Setting small goals:**

  Start each day by completing one small goal. Whether it involves writing or responding to an e-mail, finishing a presentation, or booking a meeting, the most important thing is that you commit to getting it done. To give you confidence and satisfaction, check the goal off your list once you've completed it.

- **Mixing up your habits:**

  Once a day try to break up your habits and routines by taking a different approach. For example, walk a different way to work, eat something unexpected, or perform a task with your non-dominant hand.

SOCIAL INTELLIGENCE

Looks Like . . .

Your **social intelligence** refers to your ability to readily notice and understand the emotions and intentions of both yourself and others. In addition, you're able to use this information to navigate your social world more effectively, and regulate your own emotions and behaviors.[1]

At Your Best . . .

You excel at work when your intelligence can be applied in useful and beneficial ways during group encounters.[2] For example, you enjoy helping colleagues to build or mend relationships, as well as talking to colleagues to help them feel more comfortable when confronting challenges.[3]

Challenged By . . .

Because you enjoy figuring people out, you get bored in environments where you feel you're surrounded by people who lack complexity in their expressions and relationships,[4] or who are highly similar to each other in these respects.

Shadow Side . . .

It's important not to use your social intelligence to act as an armchair psychologist where you overanalyze the emotions and motivations of others to prove your own value rather than to form a genuine connection with them.

Develop By . . .

- **Helping others feel safe:**

  Notice when people around you are experiencing stress or uncertainty. Consider the emotions they might be feeling and why they're experiencing them. Slow down to help them express and work through their uncertainty more comfortably and productively.

- **Tuning into positive emotion:**

  Pay attention to when you or those around you are experiencing high levels of engagement and energy. Savor and appreciate these moments, and think about what you can do to build upon and recreate these positive experiences in the future.

- **Noticing what motivates your team to act:**

  Each day make a note of what motivates at least one of your colleagues. Tap into these motivators and use them to frame your desired business outcomes in a way that is meaningful to your team members.

SPIRITUALITY

Looks Like . . .

Your **spirituality** refers to the strong beliefs you hold about the universe's greater purpose, and your personal understanding of your own place in the world.[1] It's these beliefs that influence your sense of meaning and purpose at work.[2]

At Your Best . . .

You thrive at work when you're able to participate in projects and tasks that connect with your sense of meaning.[3] This connection might be fostered when you feel there is an alignment between your own values and the values promoted by your workplace, when you're able to use the things you believe in to inform your work, or when you feel your work is having a widespread impact.[4]

Challenged By . . .

You find it difficult to work in situations where you struggle to uncover the meaning in what you're doing; or when you must work on a project that conflicts with your values and sense of purpose.[5] For example, if you have a strong concern for the environment, you might feel frustrated when a project wastes natural resources like paper or energy.

Shadow Side . . .

If you become too fanatical about your sense of purpose, you may find it difficult to know when to slow down, leading you and your teammates to burnout.[6] You can become so motivated by your sense of meaning and the ambition to execute your desired reality that you lose your sense of perspective. This can lead you to make unwise decisions by taking risks without weighing the options, and to pursue visions that are unfeasible or not a priority within your organization.

Develop By . . .

- **Finding your "why":**

  Be clear on what gets you out of bed each morning by completing this sentence: *Everything I do is to _____ so that _____.*[7] For example, "Everything I do is to bring out the best in myself and others, so that the world will be a better place."

- **Crafting your job:**

  Re-design your job description so it has more meaning. Focus more of your time on the tasks and people that align with your values and purpose. More at jobcrafting.org.

- **Searching for meaning in small tasks:**

  Each day find meaning in the mundane by looking at a task you're dreading or delaying, and spend a few minutes asking, "*What is the purpose of this task? What will I accomplish? Who does it help?*" Keep repeating these questions for each answer you write down until you arrive at one that makes you feel like you're engaging in something worthwhile.[8]

TEAMWORK

Looks Like . . .

Teamwork refers to your sense of belonging and commitment to a team or a greater good. You exhibit strong allegiance to the teams that you're a part of, and always endeavor to make a fair contribution when working in group contexts.[1] You orient yourself toward helping your team to achieve the best outcomes.[2]

At Your Best . . .

You excel when you're working toward a well-defined group cause, especially when this means you have to work alongside others to get the job done.[3] For example, you might enjoy putting together a group presentation, or advocating for an idea that you think could make a positive difference in your workplace.

Challenged By . . .

Because you thrive on being collaborative, you find it challenging to work with people who show more concern for themselves than the group.[4] For example, you get frustrated by people who don't pull their own weight and rely on the rest of the team to do all of the work for them.

Shadow Side . . .

When overplayed, your strength of teamwork can manifest itself in the form of excessive patriotism.[5] This shadow side can lead you to view your team as superior to others, and to hold the blind belief that your group can do no wrong. In this way, excessive patriotism creates a barrier that restricts you from seeing the value in people outside your team. This causes you to be dismissive of out-group members, and undermines your ability to collaborate with them effectively. To dial down this shadow side, make space to step back from the team from time to time. Be willing to ask the tough questions, and make sure that you're not falling into groupthink.

Develop By . . .

- **Getting involved:**

Put your hand up to become part of a team within your organization that you respect and are inspired by. This could be a formal part of your role, or it could be something you volunteer for informally.

- **Offering to coach others:**

Formally or informally volunteer to help someone you work with to set a goal.[6] Work with them to design a pathway that will move them forward, and check in with them regularly along their journey to see how they're progressing.

- **Valuing loyalty:**

Each day, perform one act of service to a team that you're a member of and hold in high regard. Be a team player by deliberately engaging in behaviors that demonstrate your loyalty.

ZEST

Looks Like . . .

Zest describes the sense of enthusiasm and vigour[1] that you experience when engaging in any activity.[2] You're able to function at optimal levels, and you possess a strong sense of being alive.[3] You fully invest in your experiences and embrace all of the journeys that life takes you on.[4]

At Your Best . . .

You're at your best when you're given full control of a task or project that you're interested in.[5] In such circumstances, you're able to ride the wave of your own passion and energy and let it take you where you need to go to get the job done well.

Challenged By . . .

Because you thrive on energy, you falter when you're exhausted due to a lack of basic needs like adequate sleep, regular exercise,[6] or a healthy diet. This might occur, for example, if your job requires you to work long or unusual hours.

Shadow Side . . .

At times, your zest can be overwhelming to the people around you. When this happens, you'll find you're off and running on a new project you're passionate and excited about, while the rest of your team has been left behind. Others can be intimidated by your energy, as they wonder how they'll be able to keep up with you and match your drive and enthusiasm. To manage this shadow side, be mindful that sometimes slowing down gets you to the finish line sooner, as it gives you a chance to bring your team along with you.

Develop By . . .

- **Being well:**

  Make "you" time a priority. Spend time each day looking after yourself by eating, moving, and resting throughout your day to ensure you replenish your energy and avoid burnout.

- **Taking a walk near nature:**

  Make time during your workday to take a brisk walk outside to renew your sense of vitality.

- **Making time to rest:**

  In the afternoon when you feel your energy depleting, take a short nap or engage in five minutes of meditation to allow your body to restore itself.

REFERENCES

CHAPTER 1

[1] Hill, J. (2001). *How well do we know our strengths?* Paper presented at the British Psychological Society Centenary Conference, Glasgow, Scotland.

[2, 4, 18] Linley, A., Willars, J., & Biswas-Diener, R. (2010). *The strengths book: What you can do, love to do, and find it hard to do – and why it matters.* Coventry, UK: CAPP Press.

[3] Achor, S. (2010). *The happiness advantage: The seven principles of positive psychology that fuel success and performance at work.* New York, NY: Crown Publishing.

[5] Biswas-Diener, R. (2010). *Practicing positive psychology coaching: Assessment, activities and strategies for success.* Hoboken, New Jersey: John Wiley & Sons.

[6] Buckingham, M. (2007). *Go put your strengths to work: 6 powerful steps to achieve outstanding performance.* New York, NY: Free Press.

[7] Niemiec, R. M. (2014). *Mindfulness and character strengths: A practical guide to flourishing.* Cambridge, MA: Hogrefe.

[8, 19] Clifton, D. O., & Harter, J. K. (2003). Investing in strengths. In K. S. Cameron, J. E. Dutton, & R. E. Quinn (Eds.), *Positive organizational scholarship* (pp. 111-121). San Francisco, CA: Berrett-Koehler.

[9, 20, 21] Hodges, T. D., & Asplund, J. (2010). Strengths development in the workplace. In A. Linley, S. Harrington, & N. Garcea (Eds.), *Oxford handbook of positive psychology and work* (pp. 213–220). Oxford: Oxford University Press.

[10, 11] Buckingham, M., & Clifton, D. (2001). *Now discover your strengths.* New York, NY: Simon & Schuster Adult Publishing Group.

[12, 16] Shahar, T. B. (2009). *Positive leadership*. Presentation at PricewatehouseCoopers. Melbourne, Australia.

[13, 14] Peterson, C., & Seligman, M. E. P. (2004). *Character strengths and virtues: A handbook and classification*. Washington, DC: American Psychological Association Press and Oxford University Press.

[15] Seligman, M. E. P. (2002). *Authentic happiness: Using the new positive psychology to realize your potential for lasting fulfillment*. New York, NY: Simon & Schuster.

[17] Kohn, A. (2014, July 25). Perfect, it turns out, is what practice doesn't make [Web blog post]. Retrieved from http://www.psychologytoday.com/blog/the-homework-myth/201407/perfect-it-turns-out-is-what-practice-doesnt-make.

CHAPTER 2

[1] Ratey, J. J. (2008). *Spark: The revolutionary new science of exercise and the brain*. New York, NY: Hachette Book Group USA.

[2] Bradberry, T. (2014, June 2). How successful people stay calm. *Forbes Online*. Retrieved August 8, 2014, from http://www.forbes.com/sites/travisbradberry/2014/02/06/how-successful-people-stay-calm/.

[3] Fredrickson, B. (2009). *Positivity: Groundbreaking research reveals how to embrace the hidden strength of positive emotions, overcome negativity, and thrive*. New York, NY: Crown Publishers.

[4] Warrell, M. (2013, June 12). How to stop stressing yourself out. *Forbes Online*. Retrieved August 10, 2014, from http://www.forbes.com/sites/margiewarrell/2013/06/12/stressed-out-turn-stress-to-your-advantage/.

[5] Seligman, M., Steen, T., Park, N., & Peterson, C. (2005). Positive psychology progress: Empirical validation of interventions. *American Psychologist, 60*, 410–421.

[6] Gander, F., Proyer, R. T., Ruch, W., & Wyss, T. (2012). The good character at work: An initial study on the contribution of character strengths in identifying healthy and unhealthy work-related behavior and experience patterns. *International Archives of Occupational and Environmental Health, 85*(8), 895-904.

[7] Mitchell, J., Stanimirovic, R., Klein, B., & Vella-Brodrick, D. (2009). A randomised controlled trial of a self-guided internet intervention promoting well-being. *Computers in Human Behavior, 25*(3), 749-760.

[8] Govindji, R., & Linley, P. A. (2007). Strengths use, self-concordance and well-being: Implications for strengths coaching and coaching psychologists. *International Coaching Psychology Review, 2* (2), 143-153.

[9] Leontopoulou, S., & Triliva, S. (2012). Explorations of subjective wellbeing and character strengths among a Greek University student sample. *International Journal of Wellbeing, 2* (3), 251-270.

[10] Proctor, C., Maltby, J., & Linley, A. (2009) Strengths use as a predictor of well-being and health- related quality of life. *Journal of Happiness Studies, 10*, 583-630.

[11] Wood, A. M., Linley, P. A., Maltby, J., Kashdan, T. B., & Hurling, R. (2010). Using personal and psychological strengths leads to increases in well-being over time: A longitudinal study and the development of the strengths use questionnaire. *Personality and Individual Differences, 50*, 15-19.

[12] Park, N., & Peterson, C. (2009). Character strengths: Research and practice. *Journal of College and Character, 10* (4), 1-10.

[13, 15, 16] Park, N., Peterson, C., & Seligman, M. E. P. (2004). Strengths of character and well-being. *Journal of social and Clinical Psychology, 23*(5), 603-619.

[14] Proyer, R. T., Gander, F., Wellenzohn, S., & Ruch, W. (2013). What good are character strengths beyond subjective well-being? The contribution of the good character on self-reported health-oriented behavior, physical fitness, and the subjective health status. *The Journal of Positive Psychology, 8*(3), 222-232.

[17] Proyer, R. T., Gander, F., Wyss, T., & Ruch, W. (2011). The relation of character strengths to past, present, and future life satisfaction among German-speaking women. *Applied Psychology: Health and Well-Being, 3*(3), 370-384.

[18] Buschor, C., Proyer, R. T., & Ruch, W. (2013). Self- and peer-rated character strengths: How do they relate to satisfaction with life and orientations to happiness? *Journal of Positive Psychology, 8* (2), 116-127.

[19] Brdar, I., & Kashdan, T. B. (2010). Character strengths and well-being in Croatia: An empirical investigation of structure and correlates. *Journal of Research in Personality, 44*, 151-154.

[20] Proyer, R. T., Ruch, W., & Buschor, C. (2012). Testing strengths-based interventions: A preliminary study on the effectiveness of a program targeting curiosity, gratitude, hope, humor, and zest for enhancing life satisfaction. *Journal of Happiness Studies, 14*(1), 275-292.

[21] Gallup. (2013). *Gallup-Healthways Well-Being Index 2013*. Retrieved from http://info.healthways.com/wbi2013.

[22] Rath, T. (2007). *Strengths Finder 2.0*. New York, NY: Gallup Press.

[23] Harter, J. K., Schmidt, F. L., & Keyes, C. L. (2003). Well-being in the workplace and its relationship to business outcomes: A review of the Gallup studies. In C. L. Keyes & J. Haidt (Eds.), *Flourishing: Positive psychology and the life well-lived* (pp. 205-224), Washington, D.C.: American Psychological Association.

[24] Haidt, J. (2006). *The happiness hypothesis: Finding modern truth in ancient wisdom*. New York, NY: Basic Books.

[25] Kay, K., & Shipman, C. (2014). *The confidence code: The science and art of self-Assurance - what women should know.* New York, NY: HarperCollins.

[26] Govindji, R., & Linley, A. (2007). Strengths use, self-concordance and well-being: Implications for strengths coaching and coaching psychologists. *International Coaching Psychology Review, 2* (2), 143-153.

[27, 45] Minhas, G. (2010). Developing realized and unrealized strengths: Implications for engagement, self-esteem, life satisfaction and well-being. *Assessment and Development Matters, 2,* 12-16.

[28] Hodges, T. D., & Harter, J. K. (2005). The quest for strengths: A review of the theory and research underlying the StrengthsQuest program for students. *educational HORIZONS, 83,* 190-201.

[29] Kirschenbaum, D. S., Ordman, A. M., Tomarken, A. J., & Holtzbauer, R. (1982). Effects of differential self-monitoring and level of mastery on sports performance: Brain power bowling. *Cognitive Therapy and Research, 6*(3), 335-341.

[30] Dubreuil, P., Forest, J., & Courcy, F. (2013). From strengths use to work performance: The role of harmonious passion, subjective vitality and concentration. *Journal of Positive Psychology.* DOI: http://dx.doi.org/10.1 080/17439760.2014.898318.

[31] Harzer, C., & Ruch, W. (2014). The role of character strengths for task performance, job dedication, interpersonal facilitation, and organizational support. *Human Performance, 27*(3), 183-205.

[32] Littman-Ovadia, H., & Steger, M. (2010). Character strengths and well-being among volunteers and employees: Toward an integrative model. *The Journal of Positive Psychology, 5*(6), 419-430.

[33] Wrzesniewski, A., McCauley, C., Rozin, P., & Schwartz, B. (1997). Jobs, careers, and callings: People's relations to their work. *Journal of Research in Personality, 31*(1), 21-33.

[34] Harzer, C., & Ruch, W. (2012). When the job is a calling: The role of applying one's signature strengths at work. *The Journal of Positive Psychology, 7*(5), 362-371.

[35] Harzer, C., & Ruch, W. (2013). The application of signature character strengths and positive experiences at work. *Journal of Happiness Studies, 14*(3), 965-983.

[36] Peterson, C., Stephens, J. P., Park, N., Lee, F., & Seligman, M. E. P. (2010). Strengths of character and work. In Linley, A., Harrington, S., & Garcea, N. (Eds.). *Oxford handbook of positive psychology and work* (pp. 221-231). New York: Oxford University Press.

[37] Littman-Ovadia, H., & Davidovitch, N. (2010). Effects of congruence and character-strength deployment on work adjustment and well-being. *International Journal of Business and Social Science, 1*(3), 138-146.

[38, 40, 41, 50] Gallup. (2013). *State of the American workplace.* Retrieved August 24, 2014, from http://www.gallup.com/strategicconsulting/163007/state-american- workplace.aspx.

[39] Gallup, (2013). *The State of the global workplace: Employee engagement insights for business leaders worldwide.* Retrieved August 24, 2014, from http://www.gallup.com/strategicconsulting/164735/state-global-workplace.aspx.

[42, 43, 48] Clifton, D. O., & Harter, J. K. (2003). Investing in strengths. In K. S. Cameron, J. E. Dutton, & R. E. Quinn (Eds.), *Positive organizational scholarship* (pp. 111-121). San Francisco, CA: Berrett-Koehler.

[44] Crabb, S. (2011). The use of coaching principles to foster employee engagement. *The Coaching Psychologist, 7*(1), 27-34.

[46] Corporate Leadership Council. (2004). *Driving performance and retention through employee engagement.* Washington, DC: Corporate Executive Board.

[47] Hodges, T. D., & Asplund, J. (2010). Strengths development in the workplace. In A. Linley, S. Harrington, & N. Garcea (Eds.), *Oxford handbook of positive psychology and work* (pp. 213–220). Oxford: Oxford University Press.

[49] Harter, J. K., Schmidt, F. L., & Hayes, T. L. (2002). Business- unit-level relationship between employee satisfaction, employee engagement, and business outcomes: A meta- analysis. *Journal of Applied Psychology, 87,* 268–279.

[51, 52] Biswas-Diener, R., Kashdan, T. B., & Minhas, G. (2011). A dynamic approach to psychological strength development and intervention. *The Journal of Positive Psychology, 6*(2), 106-118.

CHAPTER 3

[1] Baumeister, R. F., Bratslavsky, E., Finkenauer, C., & Vohs, K. D. (2001). Bad is stronger than good. *Review of General Psychology, 5*(4), 323.

[2] Hill, J. (2001). *How well do we know our strengths?* Paper presented at the British Psychological Society Centenary Conference, Glasgow, Scotland.

[3] Hodges, T. D., & Asplund, J. (2010). Strengths development in the workplace. In P. A. Linley, S. Harrington, & N. Garcea (Eds.), *Oxford handbook of positive psychology and work* (pp. 213–220). Oxford: Oxford University Press.

[4] Buckingham, M. (2007). *Go put your strengths to work: 6 powerful steps to achieve outstanding performance.* New York, NY: Free Press.

[5] Linley, A. (2008). *Average to A+: Realizing strengths in yourself and others.* Coventry, UK: CAPP Press.

[6] Anders, G. (2014). Need a career tuneup? Gallup's Tom Rath has a quiz for you. *Forbes Online.* Retrieved August 11, 2014, from http://www. forbes.com/sites/georgeanders/2013/09/04/how-gallup-hit-a-goldmine-with-strengthsfinder/ .

[7, 8, 9, 10, 11, 12] Buckingham, M., & Clifton, D. (2001). *Now discover your strengths.* New York, NY: Simon & Schuster Adult Publishing Group.

[13] Rath, T., & Conchie, B. (2009). *Strengths based leadership.* New York, NY: Gallup Press.

[14] Niemiec, R. (2013). VIA Survey or StrengthsFinder? *Psychology Today.* Retrieved August 11, 2014, from http://www.psychologytoday.com/blog/what-matters-most/201312/survey-or-strengthsfinder.

[15] Peterson, C., & Seligman, M. E. P. (2004). *Character strengths and virtues: A handbook and classification.* Washington, DC: American Psychological Association Press and Oxford University Press.

[16] Shryack, J., Steger, M. F., Krueger, R. F., & Kallie, C. S. (2010). The structure of virtue: An empirical investigation of the dimensionality of the virtues in action inventory of strengths. *Personality and Individual Differences, 48*(6), 714-719.

[17] Harzer, C., & Ruch, W. (2013). The application of signature character strengths and positive experiences at work. *Journal of Happiness Studies, 14*(3), 965-983.

[18] Peterson, C. (2008). *Character strengths.* Retrieved from University of Pennsylvania, Masters of Applied Positive Psychology.

[19] Fredrickson, B. (2009). *Positivity: Groundbreaking research reveals how to embrace the hidden strength of positive emotions, overcome negativity, and thrive.* New York, NY: Crown Publishers.

[20] Niemiec, R. M. (2013). VIA character strengths: Research and practice (The first 10 years). In H. H. Knoop & A. Delle Fave (Eds.), *Well-being and cultures: Perspectives on positive psychology* (pp. 11-30). New York: Springer.

[21] Linley, A. (2010). Realise2: Technical report. Coventry, UK: CAPP Press.

[22] Linley, A., Willars, J., & Biswas-Diener, R. (2010). *The strengths book: What you can do, love to do, and find it hard to do – and why it matters.* Coventry, UK: CAPP Press.

[23] Center for Applied Positive Psychology. (2014). *Realise2*. Retrieved August 17, 2014, from: http://www.cappeu.com/realise2.aspx.

[24] Biswas-Diener, R., Kashdan, T. B., & Minhas, G. (2011). A dynamic approach to psychological strength development and intervention. *The Journal of Positive Psychology, 6*(2), 106-118.

[25] Kaiser, R. B., & Overfield, D. V. (2011). Strengths, strengths overused, and lopsided leadership. *Consulting Psychology Journal: Practice and Research, 63*(2), 89-109.

CHAPTER 4

[1] Csikszentmihalyi, M. (1991). *Flow: The psychology of optimal experience.* New York, NY: HarperPerennial.

[2] Peterson, C. (2006). *A primer in positive psychology.* Oxford, UK: Oxford University Press.

[3] Lyubomirsky, S. (2008). *The how of happiness: A scientific approach to getting the life you want.* New York, NY: Penguin.

[4, 7, 8] Buckingham, M. (2007). *Go put your strengths to work: 6 powerful steps to achieve outstanding performance.* New York, NY: Free Press.

[5] Ericsson, K. A., Krampe, R. T., & Tesch-Römer, C. (1993). The role of deliberate practice in the acquisition of expert performance. *Psychological Review, 100*(3), 363-406.

[6] Buckingham, M., & Clifton, D. (2001). *Now discover your strengths.* New York, NY: Simon & Schuster Adult Publishing Group.

[9, 10] Niemiec, C. P., Ryan, R. M., & Deci, E. L. (2009). The path taken: Consequences of attaining intrinsic and extrinsic aspirations in post-college life. *Journal of Research in Personality, 43*, 291-306.

[11] Wrzesniewski, A., McCauley, C., Rozin, P., & Schwartz, B. (1997). Jobs, careers, and callings: People's relations to their work. *Journal of research in personality, 31*(1), 21-33.

[12] Sinek, S. (2011). *Start with why: How great leaders inspire everyone to take action.* New York, NY: Penguin Group.

[13] King, L. A. (2001). The health benefits of writing about life goals. *Personality and Social Psychology Bulletin, 27*(7), 798-807.

[14, 17] Cooperrider, D. L. (1990). Positive image, positive action: The affirmative basis of organizing. In S. Srivastva & D. Cooperrider (Eds.), *Appreciative management and leadership: The power of positive thought and action in organizations.* John Wiley & Sons.

[15] Kashdan, T. (2009). *Curious?: Discover the missing ingredient to a fulfilling life.* New York, NY: HarperCollins.

[16] Wind, Y., & Crook, C. (2005). *The power of impossible thinking.* Upper Saddle River, NI: Wharton School Publishing.

[18] Seligman, M. E. P. (2014, February 7). Prospection: The psychology of foresight. Fourth Australian Positive Psychology and Wellbeing Conference. Melbourne, Australia.

[19] Warrell, M. (2012). *Stop playing safe: Rethink risk. Unlock the power of courage. Achieve outstanding success.* New York, NY: John Wiley & Sons.

CHAPTER 5

[1] Ryan, R. M., & Deci, E. L. (2006). Self-regulation and the problem of human autonomy: Does psychology need choice, self-determination, and will? *Journal of Personality, 74*(6), 1557-1586.

[2, 3, 5, 6, 10, 24] Lopez, S. (2013) *Making hope happen: Create the future you want for yourself and others.* New York, NY: Simon & Schuster.

[4] Snyder, C. R. (2000). *Handbook of hope: Theory, measures, and applications.* United States: Academic Press.

[7, 8] Dweck, C. (2007). *Mindset: The new psychology of success.* New York, NY: Ballantine Books.

[9] Reivich, K., & Shatté, A. (2002). *The resilience factor: 7 essential skills for overcoming life's inevitable obstacles.* New York, NY: Broadway Books.

[11] Schwartz, C. E., & Sprangers, M. A. (1999). Methodological approaches for assessing response shift in longitudinal health-related quality-of-life research. *Social science & medicine, 48*(11), 1531-1548.

[12, 17, 21, 22, 23] Lyubomirsky, S. (2008). *The how of happiness: A scientific approach to getting the life you want.* New York, NY: The Penguin Press.

[13, 18, 19] Achor, S. (2010). *The happiness advantage: The seven principles of positive psychology that fuel success and performance at work.* New York, NY: Crown Publishing.

[14, 15] Brown, S. L. (2009). *Play: How it shapes the brain, opens the imagination, and invigorates the soul.* New York, NY: Penguin.

[16] Ben-Shahar, T. (2007). *Happier: Learn the secrets to daily joy and lasting fulfillment.* New York, NY: McGraw-Hill Companies.

[20] Fredrickson, B. (2009). *Positivity: Groundbreaking research reveals how to embrace the hidden strength of positive emotions, overcome negativity, and thrive.* New York, NY: Crown Publishers.

CHAPTER 6

[1] Heath, C., & Heath, D. (2010). *Switch: How to change when change is hard.* New York, NY: Random House.

[2] Neal, D. T., Wood, W., & Quinn, J. M. (2006). Habits—A repeat performance. *Current Directions in Psychological Science, 15*(4), 198-202.

[3] Baumeister, R. F., & Tierney, J. (2011). *Willpower: Rediscovering the greatest human strength.* New York, NY: Penguin.

[4] Graybiel, A. M. (1998). The basal ganglia and chunking of action repertoires. *Neurobiology of learning and memory, 70*(1), 119-136.

[5, 7, 12] Duhigg, C. (2012). *The power of habit: Why we do what we do in life and business.* New York, NY: Random House.

[6, 8] Achor, S. (2010). *The happiness advantage: The seven principles of positive psychology that fuel success and performance at work.* New York, NY: Crown Publishing.

[9] Lally, P., Van Jaarsveld, C. H., Potts, H. W., & Wardle, J. (2010). How are habits formed: Modelling habit formation in the real world. *European Journal of Social Psychology, 40*(6), 998-1009.

[10] Fredrickson, B. (2009). *Positivity: Groundbreaking research reveals how to embrace the hidden strength of positive emotions, overcome negativity, and thrive.* New York, NY: Crown Publishers.

[11] Greenberg, M., & Maymin, S. (2013). *Profit from the positive: Proven leadership strategies to boost productivity and transform your business.* New York, NY: McGraw Hill Professional.

[13, 14, 17] Wrzesniewski, A. (2014). Engage in job crafting. In J. E. Dutton & G. M. Spreitzer (Eds.), *How to be a positive leader: Small actions, big impact.* San Francisco, CA: Berrett-Koehler.

[15] Rath, T., Harter, J., & Harter, J. K. (2010). *Wellbeing: The five essential elements.* New York, NY: Gallup Press.

[16] Ben-Shahar, T. (2007). Happier: Learn the secrets to daily joy and lasting fulfillment. New York, NY: McGraw-Hill Companies.

[18] Lyubomirsky, S. (2013). *The myths of happiness: What should make you happy, but doesn't, what shouldn't make you happy, but does.* New York, NY: Penguin.

[19] Duckworth, A. L., Peterson, C., Matthews, M. D., & Kelly, D. R. (2007). Grit: Perseverance and passion for long-term goals. *Journal of Personality and Social Psychology, 92*(6), 1087-1101.

[20] Duckworth, A. Research Statement. *The Duckworth Lab,* 2014. Retrieved August 25, 2014 from https://sites.sas.upenn.edu/duckworth/pages/research-statement.

[21] Damon, W. (2008). *The path to purpose: Helping our children find their calling in life.* New York, NY: Simon and Schuster.

[22, 24, 25] Duckworth, A. (2014, August 5). How grit enables us to show up, shine & succeed at work [Online interview]. Retrieved from www.michellemcquaid.com/showupshineandsucceed/listen.

[23] Ericsson, K. A., Krampe, R. T., & Tesch-Römer, C. (1993). The role of deliberate practice in the acquisition of expert performance. *Psychological Review, 100*(3), 363-406.

CHAPTER 7

[1, 9] Cooperrider, D. L., & McQuaid, M. (2012). The positive arc of systemic strengths: How appreciative inquiry and sustainable designing can bring out the best in human systems. *Journal of Corporate Citizenship, 46,* 71-102.

[2] Vaillant, G. E. (2012). *Triumphs of experience: The men of the Harvard Grant Study.* Boston: Harvard University Press.

[3] Dutton, J. E., & Heaphy, E. D. (2003). The power of high-quality connections. *Positive organizational scholarship: Foundations of a new discipline, 3,* 263-278.

[4] Rath, T., Harter, J., & Harter, J. K. (2010). *Wellbeing: The five essential elements.* New York, NY: Gallup Press.

[5, 15] Fredrickson, B. (2009). *Positivity: Groundbreaking research reveals how to embrace the hidden strength of positive emotions, overcome negativity, and thrive.* New York, NY: Crown Publishers.

[6] Fredrickson, B. L. (2013). *Love 2.0: Finding happiness and health in moments of connection.* New York, NY: Penguin.

[7] Linley, A. (2008). *Average to A+: Realizing strengths in yourself and others.* Coventry, UK: CAPP Press.

[8] Duncan, R. D. (2013, August 20). Nine ways to keep your company's most valuable asset – Its employees. *Forbes Online*. Retrieved August 10, 2014, from http://www.forbes.com/sites/forbesleadershipforum/2013/08/20/nine-ways-to-keep-your-companys-most-valuable-asset-its-employees/.

[10, 11, 12] Cooperrider, D., & Whitney, D. D. (2005). *Appreciative inquiry: A positive revolution in change*. San Franscico, CA: Berrett-Koehler Publishers.

[13] Gorey, A. (2012, March 26). Who are you really hiring? 10 shocking HR statistics. *HR.com*. Retrieved August 10, 2014, from http://www.hr.com/en/app/blog/2012/03/who-are-you-really-hiring-10-shocking-hr-statistic_h09y2ol0.html.

[14] Wei, W. (2010, October 26). Tony Hsieh: Bad hires have cost Zappos over $100 million. *Business Insider Australia*. Retrieved August 10, 2014, from http://www.businessinsider.com.au/tony-hsieh-making-the-right-hires-2010-10.

[16] Bersin, J. (2014, February 4). Spending on corporate training soars: Employee capabilities now a priority. Retrieved August 10, 2014, from http://www.forbes.com/sites/joshbersin/2014/02/04/the-recovery-arrives-corporate-training-spend-skyrockets/.

[17] Smith, J. (2013, November 13). How to show appreciation and get better results from your employees this holiday season. Retrieved August 10, 2014, from http://www.forbes.com/sites/jacquelynsmith/2013/11/13/how-to-show-appreciation-and-get-better-results-from-your-employees-this-holiday-season/.

APPRECIATION OF BEAUTY & EXCELLENCE

[1] Peterson, C., & Seligman, M. E. P. (2004). *Character strengths and virtues: A handbook and classification*. Washington, DC: American Psychological Association Press and Oxford University Press.

[2,3] Positive Leadership Pty Ltd. (2008). *VIA Signature Strengths Cards*. Purchased from http://www.positiveleadership.com.au/page/via_cards.html.

BRAVERY

[1] VIA Institute. (2014). *Bravery*. Retrieved from http://www.viacharacter. org/www/Character-Strengths/Bravery; Shelp, E. E. (1984). Courage: A neglected virtue in the patient-physician relation. *Social Science and Medicine, 18*(4), 351-360.

[2] Shelp, E. E. (1984). Courage: A neglected virtue in the patient-physician relation. *Social Science and Medicine, 18*(4), 351-360.

[3] Peterson, C., & Seligman, M. E. P. (2004). *Character strengths and virtues: A handbook and classification.* Washington, DC: American Psychological Association Press and Oxford University Press.

[4,7] VIA Institute. (2014). *Bravery*. Retrieved from http://www.viacharacter. org/www/Character-Strengths/Bravery.

[5] Positive Leadership Pty Ltd. (2008). *VIA Signature Strengths Cards*. Purchased from http://www.positiveleadership.com.au/page/via_cards.html.

[6] Seligman, M. E. P. (2014). Chris Peterson's unfinished masterwork: The real mental illnesses. *The Journal of Positive Psychology.* doi:10.1080/1743 9760.2014.888582.

CREATIVITY

[1] Peterson, C., & Seligman, M. E. P. (2004). *Character strengths and virtues: A handbook and classification.* Washington, DC: American Psychological Association Press and Oxford University Press.

[2,3] Positive Leadership Pty Ltd. (2008). *VIA Signature Strengths Cards*. Purchased from http://www.positiveleadership.com.au/page/via_cards.html.

CURIOSITY

[1] Peterson, C., & Seligman, M. E. P. (2004). *Character strengths and virtues: A handbook and classification*. Washington, DC: American Psychological Association Press and Oxford University Press.

[2, 3] Positive Leadership Pty Ltd. (2008). *VIA Signature Strengths Cards*. Purchased from http://www.positiveleadership.com.au/page/via_cards.html.

FAIRNESS

[1] Peterson, C., & Seligman, M. E. P. (2004). *Character strengths and virtues: A handbook and classification*. Washington, DC: American Psychological Association Press and Oxford University Press.

[2, 3] Positive Leadership Pty Ltd. (2008). *VIA Signature Strengths Cards*. Purchased from http://www.positiveleadership.com.au/page/via_cards.html.

[4] Seligman, M. E. P. (2014). Chris Peterson's unfinished masterwork: The real mental illnesses. *The Journal of Positive Psychology*. doi:10.1080/1743 9760.2014.888582.

[5] VIA Institute. (2014). *Fairness*. Retrieved from http://www.viacharacter. org/www/Character-Strengths/Fairness.

FORGIVENESS

[1] Peterson, C., & Seligman, M. E. P. (2004). *Character strengths and virtues: A handbook and classification*. Washington, DC: American Psychological Association Press and Oxford University Press.

[2] McCullough, M. E. (2000). Forgiveness as human strength: Theory, measurement, and links to well-being. *Journal of Social and Clinical Psychology, 19*(1), 43-55.

[3, 4] Positive Leadership Pty Ltd. (2008). *VIA Signature Strengths Cards.* Purchased from http://www.positiveleadership.com.au/page/via_cards.html.

[5] Seligman, M. E. P. (2014). Chris Peterson's unfinished masterwork: The real mental illnesses. *The Journal of Positive Psychology.* doi:10.1080/1743 9760.2014.888582.

[6] VIA Institute. (2014). *Forgiveness.* Retrieved from http://www. viacharacter.org/www/Character-Strengths/Forgiveness.

GRATITUDE

[1] Peterson, C., & Seligman, M. E. P. (2004). *Character strengths and virtues: A handbook and classification.* Washington, DC: American Psychological Association Press and Oxford University Press.

[2, 4] Positive Leadership Pty Ltd. (2008). *VIA Signature Strengths Cards.* Purchased from http://www.positiveleadership.com.au/page/via_cards.html.

[3] Eammons, R. (2003). Acts of gratitude in organizations. In K. S. Cameron, J. E. Dutton, & R. E. Quinn (Eds.), *Positive Organizational Scholarship* (pp. 81-93), San Francisco: Berrett-Koehler.

[5] Seligman, M. E. P. (2014). Chris Peterson's unfinished masterwork: The real mental illnesses. *The Journal of Positive Psychology.* doi:10.1080/1743 9760.2014.888582.

HONESTY

[1] Peterson, C., & Seligman, M. E. P. (2004). *Character strengths and virtues: A handbook and classification.* Washington, DC: American Psychological Association Press and Oxford University Press.

[2, 3] Positive Leadership Pty Ltd. (2008). *VIA Signature Strengths Cards.* Purchased from http://www.positiveleadership.com.au/page/via_cards.html.

[4] Seligman, M. E. P. (2014). Chris Peterson's unfinished masterwork: The real mental illnesses. *The Journal of Positive Psychology*. doi:10.1080/1743 9760.2014.888582.

HOPE

[1] Peterson, C., & Seligman, M. E. P. (2004). *Character strengths and virtues: A handbook and classification.* Washington, DC: American Psychological Association Press and Oxford University Press.

[2, 4] Positive Leadership Pty Ltd. (2008). *VIA Signature Strengths Cards.* Purchased from http://www.positiveleadership.com.au/page/via_cards.html.

[3, 6] Snyder, C. R. (2002). Hope theory: Rainbows in the mind. *Psychological Inquiry, 13*(4), 249-275.

[5] Seligman, M. E. P. (2014). Chris Peterson's unfinished masterwork: The real mental illnesses. *The Journal of Positive Psychology*. doi:10.1080/1743 9760.2014.888582.

[7, 8] Lopez, S. (2013). *Making hope happen: Create the future you want for yourself and others.* New York, NY: Simon & Schuster.

[9] Lopez, S. (2013). *Hope how-tos.* Retrieved from http://www.hopemonger. com/about/hope-how-tos.

HUMILITY

[1, 3] Tangney, J. P. (2000). Humility: Theoretical perspectives, empirical findings and directions for future research. *Journal of Social and Clinical Psychology, 19*(1), 70-82.

[2, 6] VIA Institute. (2014). *Humility.* Retrieved from http://www.viacharacter. org/www/Character-Strengths/Humility.

[4] Positive Leadership Pty Ltd. (2008). *VIA Signature Strengths Cards.* Purchased from http://www.positiveleadership.com.au/page/via_cards.html.

[5] Seligman, M. E. P. (2014). Chris Peterson's unfinished masterwork: The real mental illnesses. *The Journal of Positive Psychology.* doi:10.1080/1743 9760.2014.888582.

HUMOR

[1,3] Peterson, C., & Seligman, M. E. P. (2004). *Character strengths and virtues: A handbook and classification.* Washington, DC: American Psychological Association Press and Oxford University Press.

[2,4] Positive Leadership Pty Ltd. (2008). *VIA Signature Strengths Cards.* Purchased from http://www.positiveleadership.com.au/page/via_cards.html.

[5] Gostick, A., & Christopher, S. (2008). *The levity effect: Why it pays to lighten up.* Hoboken, NJ: Wiley.

JUDGMENT

[1] Peterson, C., & Seligman, M. E. P. (2004). *Character strengths and virtues: A handbook and classification.* Washington, DC: American Psychological Association Press and Oxford University Press.

[2] Positive Leadership Pty Ltd. (2008). *VIA Signature Strengths Cards.* Purchased from http://www.positiveleadership.com.au/page/via_cards.html.

[3] Schwartz, B., Ward, A., Monterosso, J., Lyubomirsky, S., White, K., & Lehman, D. R. (2002). Maximizing versus satisficing: Happiness is a matter of choice. *Journal of Personality and Social Psychology, 83*(5), 1178-1197.

[4] VIA Institute. (2014). *Judgment.* Retrieved from http://www.viacharacter.org/www/Character-Strengths/Judment.

KINDNESS

[1, 6, 7] VIA Institute. (2014). *Kindness*. Retrieved from http://www. viacharacter.org/www/Character-Strengths/Kindness.

[2] Peterson, C., & Seligman, M. E. P. (2004). *Character strengths and virtues: A handbook and classification*. Washington, DC: American Psychological Association Press and Oxford University Press.

[3] Positive Leadership Pty Ltd. (2008). *VIA Signature Strengths Cards*. Purchased from http://www.positiveleadership.com.au/page/via_cards.html.

[4] Grant, A. M. (2013). *Give and take: A revolutionary approach to success*. New York, NY: Viking Press.

[5] Dutton, as cited in McQuaid, M. (2014). *Does compassion have value at work?* [Web blog post]. Retrieved from http://www.michellemcquaid. com/compassion/.

LEADERSHIP

[1] Peterson, C., & Seligman, M. E. P. (2004). *Character strengths and virtues: A handbook and classification*. Washington, DC: American Psychological Association Press and Oxford University Press.

[2] VIA Institute. (2014). *Leadership*. Retrieved from http://www. viacharacter.org/www/Character-Strengths/Leadership.

[3] Bass, B. M. (1990). From transactional to transformational leadership: Learning to share the vision. *Organizational Dynamics, 18*(3), 19-31.

[4] Positive Leadership Pty Ltd. (2008). *VIA Signature Strengths Cards*. Purchased from http://www.positiveleadership.com.au/page/via_cards.html.

[5] Seligman, M. E. P. (2014). Chris Peterson's unfinished masterwork: The real mental illnesses. *The Journal of Positive Psychology*. doi:10.1080/1743 9760.2014.888582

LOVE

[1, 3] VIA Institute. (2014). *Love*. Retrieved from http://www.viacharacter.org/www/Character-Strengths/Love.

[2] Peterson, C., & Seligman, M. E. P. (2004). *Character strengths and virtues: A handbook and classification.* Washington, DC: American Psychological Association Press and Oxford University Press.

[4, 5] Positive Leadership Pty Ltd. (2008). *VIA Signature Strengths Cards.* Purchased from http://www.positiveleadership.com.au/page/via_cards.html.

LOVE OF LEARNING

[1] Peterson, C., & Seligman, M. E. P. (2004). *Character strengths and virtues: A handbook and classification.* Washington, DC: American Psychological Association Press and Oxford University Press.

[2] Positive Leadership Pty Ltd. (2008). VIA Signature Strengths Cards. Purchased from http://www.positiveleadership.com.au/page/via_cards.html.

[3] Seligman, M. E. P. (2014). Chris Peterson's unfinished masterwork: The real mental illnesses. *The Journal of Positive Psychology.* doi:10.1080/1743 9760.2014.888582.

PERSEVERANCE

[1] Peterson, C., & Seligman, M. E. P. (2004). *Character strengths and virtues: A handbook and classification.* Washington, DC: American Psychological Association Press and Oxford University Press.

[2] VIA Institute. (2014). *Perseverance*. Retrieved from http://www.viacharacter.org/www/Character-Strengths/Perseverance.

[3, 4] Positive Leadership Pty Ltd. (2008). VIA Signature Strengths Cards. Purchased from http://www.positiveleadership.com.au/page/via_cards.html.

[5] Seligman, M. E. P. (2014). Chris Peterson's unfinished masterwork: The real mental illnesses. *The Journal of Positive Psychology.* doi:10.1080/1743 9760.2014.888582.

PERSPECTIVE

[1, 4] VIA Institute. (2014). *Perspective.* Retrieved from http://www. viacharacter.org/www/Character-Strengths/Perspective.

[2, 3] Positive Leadership Pty Ltd. (2008). VIA Signature Strengths Cards. Purchased from http://www.positiveleadership.com.au/page/via_cards.html.

PRUDENCE

[1] Peterson, C., & Seligman, M. E. P. (2004). *Character strengths and virtues: A handbook and classification.* Washington, DC: American Psychological Association Press and Oxford University Press.

[2, 3] Positive Leadership Pty Ltd. (2008). VIA Signature Strengths Cards. Purchased from http://www.positiveleadership.com.au/page/via_cards.html.

[4, 5] VIA Institute. (2014). *Prudence.* Retrieved from http://www.viacharacter. org/www/Character-Strengths/Prudence.

SELF-REGULATION

[1] Peterson, C., & Seligman, M. E. P. (2004). *Character strengths and virtues: A handbook and classification.* Washington, DC: American Psychological Association Press and Oxford University Press.

[2, 3] Positive Leadership Pty Ltd. (2008). VIA Signature Strengths Cards. Purchased from http://www.positiveleadership.com.au/page/via_cards.html.

[4] Seligman, M. E. P. (2014). Chris Peterson's unfinished masterwork: The real mental illnesses. *The Journal of Positive Psychology.* doi:10.1080/1743 9760.2014.888582.

SOCIAL INTELLIGENCE

[1] Peterson, C., & Seligman, M. E. P. (2004). *Character strengths and virtues: A handbook and classification.* Washington, DC: American Psychological Association Press and Oxford University Press.

[2, 4] Positive Leadership Pty Ltd. (2008). VIA Signature Strengths Cards. Purchased from http://www.positiveleadership.com.au/page/via_cards.html.

[3] VIA Institute. (2014). *Social Intelligence.* Retrieved from http://www.viacharacter.org/www/Character-Strengths/Social-Intelligence.

SPIRITUALITY

[1] VIA Institute. (2014). *Spirituality.* Retrieved from http://www.viacharacter.org/www/Character-Strengths/Spirituality.

[2] Peterson, C., & Seligman, M. E. P. (2004). *Character strengths and virtues: A handbook and classification.* Washington, DC: American Psychological Association Press and Oxford University Press.

[3, 5] Positive Leadership Pty Ltd. (2008). *VIA Signature Strengths Cards.* Purchased from http://www.positiveleadership.com.au/page/via_cards.html.

[4] Steger, as cited in McQuaid, M. (2014). Want more meaningful work? [Web blog post]. Retrieved from http://www.michellemcquaid.com/meaningful-work/.

[6] Seligman, M. E. P. (2014). Chris Peterson's unfinished masterwork: The real mental illnesses. *The Journal of Positive Psychology.* doi:10.1080/1743 9760.2014.888582.

[7] Sinek, S. (2011). *Start with why: How great leaders inspire everyone to take action.* New York, NY: Penguin Group.

[8] Ben-Shahar, T. (2007). *Happier: Learn the secrets to daily joy and lasting fulfillment.* New York, NY: McGraw-Hill Professional.

TEAMWORK

[1] Peterson, C., & Seligman, M. E. P. (2004). *Character strengths and virtues: A handbook and classification.* Washington, DC: American Psychological Association Press and Oxford University Press.

[2,6] VIA Institute. (2014). *Teamwork.* Retrieved from http://www.viacharacter.org/www/Character-Strengths/Teamwork.

[3,4] Positive Leadership Pty Ltd. (2008). *VIA Signature Strengths Cards.* Purchased from http://www.positiveleadership.com.au/page/via_cards.html.

[5] Seligman, M. E. P. (2014). Chris Peterson's unfinished masterwork: The real mental illnesses. *The Journal of Positive Psychology.* doi:10.1080/1743 9760.2014.888582.

ZEST

[1] Ryan, R. M., & Frederick, C. (1997). On energy, personality and health: Subjective vitality as a dynamic reflection of well-being. *Journal of Personality, 65*(3), 529-565.

[2,4] VIA Institute. (2014). *Zest.* Retrieved from http://www.viacharacter.org/www/Character-Strengths/Zest.

[3] Peterson, C., & Seligman, M. E. P. (2004). *Character strengths and virtues: A handbook and classification.* Washington, DC: American Psychological Association Press and Oxford University Press.

[5,6] Positive Leadership Pty Ltd. (2008). *VIA Signature Strengths Cards.* Purchased from http://www.positiveleadership.com.au/page/via_cards.html.

WITH HEARTFELT THANKS FROM MICHELLE

I was fortunate enough to have the privilege of learning the science and art of developing strengths at the feet of the late Professor Chris Peterson. He was a giant man—big in body, heart, and mind—who filled the world with kindness, laughter, and incredible research on how to bring out the best in others and ourselves. Chris encouraged us to understand the limitations and the possibilities of the science of positive psychology and to take it into the world to make a difference. It's my sincere hope that this book will help his incredible work find its way into more lives.

Thanks must also go to my dear Professor Martin Seligman for having the courage, conviction, and commitment to put a science of human flourishing—with all the challenges it brings—center stage around the world. I am constantly inspired and grateful for your unique ability and generosity in finding, nurturing, and connecting researchers and practitioners across a myriad of domains to help mankind. You positively change lives every day—mine continues to be one of them.

This book would not be possible without the kindness of hundreds of organizations and individuals who have bravely allowed me into their workplaces and their lives to share my knowledge about strengths. Your willingness to learn, play, and share your journeys are the backbone of this book. It would not exist without you. Special thanks to Anna Phillips, Dayle Stevens, Nicole DeVine, Melitta Hardenberg, Luke Sayers, Sophie Crawford-Jones, and the team at EPA Victoria who have given such incredible opportunities to deliver this work.

This book would also not be possible without the amazing people who bring out the best in me each day professionally and personally. Special thanks to Caitlin Judd and Natalie Rudolph—you are my dream team who turn my wild dreams into reality; to my ever-patient husband, Patrick, and our constantly strength-testing children, Charlie and Jamie; to my dear friend Megan for all the wise counsel and encouragement; and to my wonderful family and friends who patiently wait for my heart strengths to sometimes kick in!

Finally, to Erin Lawn, my incredible collaborator on this book. Thank you for your prudence, perseverance, social intelligence, teamwork, and curiosity. This would never have been completed without your strengths. I'm still amazed at our journey from the classroom to the cover of this book. I'm so grateful you have more calm, grace, and courage than anyone I've ever met. Can't wait to see what comes next.

WITH HEARTFELT THANKS FROM ERIN

Firstly, I'd like to extend my thanks to Caitlin and the rest of the team for their energy and patience in helping Michelle and I to deliver our vision for this book. I would also like to thank the lovely Natalie Brain for her sincere belief in me. I will always hold onto your wise words, Natalie, and be forever grateful to have had the opportunity to learn from someone with such an immensely kind heart and vibrant spirit.

To all of the researchers who continue to add to the rich field that is the study of human flourishing—your work has provided hope and stimulated the curiosity of many young minds like my own who are energized by the opportunities and learnings that the field has to offer. Thank you for all of your fascinating and fruitful work.

I would also like to express my gratitude for the blessing of my two wonderful parents. You both inspire me so much and in so many ways. The wholehearted lovingness, encouragement, and support you have offered me at every step of my journey so far is something that I always treasure. Thank you both for being you.

Finally, I am so grateful to have been given the opportunity to collaborate with Michelle McQuaid on such an interesting and exciting project. It has been a privilege to learn from and be inspired by someone with such expertise, passion, flexibility, kindness—and most of all, zest. I will always be thankful for your mentorship, Michelle, and the ways it has helped me to grow and flourish.

ABOUT MICHELLE

Michelle McQuaid is a best-selling author, workplace wellbeing teacher, and a playful change activator. With more than a decade of senior leadership experience in large organizations around the world, Michelle is passionate about translating cutting-edge research from positive psychology and neuroscience into practical strategies for health, happiness, and business success.

An honorary fellow at Melbourne University's Graduate School of Education, her work has been featured in *Forbes*, the *Harvard Business Review*, the *Wall Street Journal*, the *Huffington Post*, *Boss Magazine*, *The Age*, *Women's Agenda*, *Wellbeing Magazine* and more.

She holds a master's in applied positive psychology from the University of Pennsylvania and is currently completing her PhD in appreciative inquiry under the supervision of David Cooperrider.

Michelle lives to help people discover their strengths, move beyond their fears, and finally discover what it truly takes to flourish with confidence.

To learn more about Michelle visit www.michellemcquaid.com.

ABOUT ERIN

Erin Lawn is currently completing her bachelor of arts degree, majoring in psychology at the University of Melbourne, and was placed on the Faculty of Arts Dean's Honors List in 2013.

Erin loves embracing her strength of curiosity to learn about the brain, mental processes, and human behavior. Through her degree, she has undertaken studies in the areas of wellbeing, performance, and positive leadership.

Erin is fascinated by the science of human flourishing and is passionate about helping others to understand and fulfill their potential. She hopes to keep using the knowledge and skills she is acquiring from her studies to help individuals, teams, and organizations to thrive.

WANT A LITTLE EXTRA HELP?

It is our heartfelt belief that this book, and the resources it connects you to, provides a wealth of ideas on how you can put your strengths to work. But if you'd like a little extra help on your journey, it's Michelle's pleasure to also offer you:

Appreciative Coaching

Are you ready to show up and shine? If so, I work one-on-one with a small group of extraordinary people (like you) to help them use their VIA strengths to build their confidence, understand what success looks like, define the pathways forward, and take the next steps to create powerful change in their work and in their lives.

Online Training

Want a step-by-step blueprint to discover, develop, and deliver on your strengths at work? Join my six-week online training program to gain the knowledge, tools, and support you need to make working with your strengths a way of life.

Keynote Speaking

If you're looking to create not just an event but also an experience that will empower people to discover their strengths and immediately put them to work, look no further. I've taught thousands of people how to use their VIA strengths to improve confidence, lower stress, and perform at their best to improve individual, team, and organizational outcomes.

If I can help in any way to move you from functioning to flourishing, I would love to hear from you! Please get in touch.

 michellemcquaid.com   chellemcquaid

Made in the USA
San Bernardino, CA
29 November 2016